CAMBRIDGE LIBRARY COLLECTION

Books of enduring scholarly value

Classics

From the Renaissance to the nineteenth century, Latin and Greek were compulsory subjects in almost all European universities, and most early modern scholars published their research and conducted international correspondence in Latin. Latin had continued in use in Western Europe long after the fall of the Roman empire as the lingua franca of the educated classes and of law, diplomacy, religion and university teaching. The flight of Greek scholars to the West after the fall of Constantinople in 1453 gave impetus to the study of ancient Greek literature and the Greek New Testament. Eventually, just as nineteenth-century reforms of university curricula were beginning to erode this ascendancy, developments in textual criticism and linguistic analysis, and new ways of studying ancient societies, especially archaeology, led to renewed enthusiasm for the Classics. This collection offers works of criticism, interpretation and synthesis by the outstanding scholars of the nineteenth century.

Itinerary of the Morea

Classical topographer Sir William Gell (1777–1836) first came to public attention with his *Topography of Troy* (1804). Based on his travels around Bunarbashi, near to where Schliemann would subsequently excavate, the work became a standard treatise. Byron even wrote: 'Of Dardan tours let dilettanti tell, / I leave topography to classic Gell.' A noted conversationalist and intellectual intermediary, Gell became a Fellow of the Royal Society and, indeed, a Member of the Society of Dilettanti. He also served, in 1803, on a diplomatic mission to the Ionian Islands; his subsequent journey, with the archaeologist Edward Dodwell, through the Peloponnese - then known as the Morea - became the subject of several later books, including *Narrative of a Journey in the Morea* (1823; also reissued in this series) and this 1817 publication. Comprising a survey of routes through the area, and their natural and archaeological landmarks, it sheds light on both contemporary Greece and the practicalities of early topographical study.

T0370646

Cambridge University Press has long been a pioneer in the reissuing of out-of-print titles from its own backlist, producing digital reprints of books that are still sought after by scholars and students but could not be reprinted economically using traditional technology. The Cambridge Library Collection extends this activity to a wider range of books which are still of importance to researchers and professionals, either for the source material they contain, or as landmarks in the history of their academic discipline.

Drawing from the world-renowned collections in the Cambridge University Library and other partner libraries, and guided by the advice of experts in each subject area, Cambridge University Press is using state-of-the-art scanning machines in its own Printing House to capture the content of each book selected for inclusion. The files are processed to give a consistently clear, crisp image, and the books finished to the high quality standard for which the Press is recognised around the world. The latest print-on-demand technology ensures that the books will remain available indefinitely, and that orders for single or multiple copies can quickly be supplied.

The Cambridge Library Collection brings back to life books of enduring scholarly value (including out-of-copyright works originally issued by other publishers) across a wide range of disciplines in the humanities and social sciences and in science and technology.

Itinerary of the Morea

*Being a Description
of the Routes of that Peninsula*

WILLIAM GELL

CAMBRIDGE UNIVERSITY PRESS

Cambridge, New York, Melbourne, Madrid, Cape Town,
Singapore, São Paolo, Delhi, Mexico City

Published in the United States of America by Cambridge University Press, New York

www.cambridge.org
Information on this title: www.cambridge.org/9781108050814

© in this compilation Cambridge University Press 2012

This edition first published 1817
This digitally printed version 2012

ISBN 978-1-108-05081-4 Paperback

This book reproduces the text of the original edition. The content and language reflect
the beliefs, practices and terminology of their time, and have not been updated.

Cambridge University Press wishes to make clear that the book, unless originally published
by Cambridge, is not being republished by, in association or collaboration with, or
with the endorsement or approval of, the original publisher or its successors in title.

The material originally positioned here is too large for reproduction in this reissue. A PDF can be downloaded from the web address given on page ivof this book, by clicking on 'Resources Available'.

Itinerary

OF

THE MOREA:

BEING

A DESCRIPTION

OF

THE ROUTES OF THAT PENINSULA.

By SIR WILLIAM GELL,

M.A. F.R.S. F.S.A.

LONDON:

PRINTED FOR RODWELL AND MARTIN,

(SUCCESSORS TO MR. FAULDER,)

NEW BOND STREET,

By S. HAMILTON, WEYBRIDGE, SURREY.

1817.

TO

M. BARBIÈ DU BOCAGE,

&c. &c. &c.

WHOSE RESEARCHES HAVE BEEN OF THE GREATEST IMPORTANCE
TO GRECIAN TOPOGRAPHY,

This Work,

CONTAINING

AN ESSAY ON THE ROUTES

OF

THE MOREA,

IS RESPECTFULLY INSCRIBED,

BY HIS FRIEND,

AND FAITHFUL SERVANT,

THE AUTHOR.

PREFACE.

To those who travel in the North of Europe, the enumeration of every rivulet, source, or habitation, which occurs on the road, must appear totally devoid of interest or utility; and the notation of tiles, broken pottery, or blocks of stone, yet more frivolous and absurd. To the Grecian traveller, however, these may be circumstances of the more importance. Almost every brook has its value to history or geography; and good water is in some districts so scarce, that he who should make known the discovery of a source, or well, upon the Sunian promontory, would not only materially assist future

travellers, but render an essential service to the na-
vigators of the Archipelago.

The prospect of arriving in a given time, even
at a hut, in so wild a country as Greece, at the close
of a day's journey, cannot be without its charm;
and the existence of a single roof may often afford
facilities for examining a district hitherto unex-
plored, on account of its distance from any well-
known village.

Blocks of stone always indicate the site of a
temple, a city, or a fortress; while the tiles are
sometimes the only memorials of a modern town
important to the history of the lower ages, or of the
wars between the Turks and Venetians, which the
perishable nature of the materials employed in its
construction have suffered to exist on the spot.

Broken pottery may also sometimes serve to point

out the sites of fortresses of the most remote ages, from which the blocks have been removed for the erection of cities of a less ancient date.

It is to be understood, that the measure of distances by the time employed on the road can only be relative, though taken by means of the same horse, always having a person walking in company. This may occasionally vary; for the same animal, returning at night to the spot whence he set out in the morning, is found to hasten his pace, so as sometimes to shorten the distance by nearly one third. This defect is in some measure remedied by a rough statement of the estimated number of miles, by the road, from one station to another: but, while the roads continue in their present state, the hours and minutes will be found of infinitely more service to the traveller; as these miles, in a mountainous country, bear no proportion to the real distances, and vary in their excess beyond the direct line between an eighth and a third.

To those who ride post through the country, neither this Essay, nor any other, can be of much use on the spot; for the route from Krabata to Argos, which is here given at 1 hour 52 minutes, might, in dry weather, with a good horse, be traversed in 30 minutes. Even to such travellers, however, the present Essay will become interesting when they publish the account of their journeys, as they may learn from it what they would have seen, had they travelled for the purpose of observation.

It has been asserted, that we are now so well acquainted with Greece, that an apology is required for any work on that country. This might be true, if any one of the critics who have enjoyed this imaginary triumph over those who have travelled in Greece had even heard the names of the towns and villages of the Morea. Our sailors may have seen about seven towns on the coast; while, with regard to the situation of ancient cities, our best scholars would be puzzled to point out the sites of Psophis, Methydrium, or Orchomenos, or even Mantinea and Tegea. It is the entire ignorance of the country which has tempted people to assert that they were thoroughly acquainted with it. The gentleman to whom this Essay is inscribed, with all the advantages he possesses of talent and research, is fully sensible of the deficiency of the materials necessary to compile a map of the country.

Notwithstanding the great number of new names and situations to be found in this volume, much yet remains to be done, particularly in Laconia, before a sufficient knowledge of the Morea be obtained. One or two individuals only possess the necessary documents; but it is to be hoped that future travellers may be induced to add to the present collection, now that the foundation is once laid.

In the orthography of names, the several different methods of spelling have been generally given, and the ancient and modern appellations have been often indiscriminately used, when well ascertained. The modern names, as well as the ancient, are frequently expressive of some local peculiarity;- and as no two persons write them alike, while some studiously spell them wrong, in order to make a difference, where none exists, between the ancient and modern Greek, it is better that a traveller should be accustomed to the several methods.

The ancient divisions are adopted, in the hope of rendering the whole more intelligible to the English reader, who must be more accustomed to them than the modern divisions. When this is not strictly observed, it is for the purpose of not breaking a connected line, or circle of routes, as from Sicyon to Alopeki, which, though in Sicyonia, was necessary to complete the tour of Achaia.

There are many words which it will be necessary for every traveller to learn, being in perpetual use for the most ordinary objects, and often compounded with proper names. On this account, an explanation of those most frequently occurring is here given :—

Derveni, a guard on the road.

Khan, an inn.

Khangi, the innkeeper.

Pyrgo, a tower, or house built like a tower.

Limne, a lake.

Bouno, or *Vouno,* a mountain.

Potamos, a river.

Pege, a well.

Kastro, a castle.

Palaio Kastro, an ancient castle.

Romaic, Roman, a name assumed by the Greeks.

Hellenic, ancient Greek.

Katabathron, pronounced by the Greeks *Katavottra,* a subterraneous passage for the water of a lake or river.

Brysse, and *Kephalo Brysse,* a source of water.

Teke, a Turkish chapel.

Kiosk, a summer-house.

Tchiftik, or *Chifflik,* a Turkish villa.

Nerro, water—added to the proper names of rivers.

Mandri, or *Mantra,* a shepherd's habitation or fold.

Stagni, a temporary shepherd's fold.

Kalybea, a temporary village, sometimes increasing to a populous and fixed town.

Metochi, a farm-house and chapel belonging to a monastery.

Agios, pronounced *Ayos,* Saint—as Agios Giorgios, St. George.

ACHAIA.

B

PATRASS.

PATRAS, called by the Italians Patrasso, and by the natives Patra, has a population of about 10,000 souls. The Turkish governor has the title of Vaivode, and there are resident consuls of the principal European States. The trade consists chiefly in currants and skins. The city, which is the see of a Greek Metropolitan, is situated on an agreeable eminence, projecting from Mount Boidia, the ancient Panachaicon, and is surrounded by vineyards. The plain on the south produces grain, olives and oranges, and is well cultivated. In it, at the distance of about a mile from the town, is a most magnificent cypress, which has assumed the form of a cedar: Spòn and Wheeler measured it, since which time it has much increased in bulk. In the walls of the castle were several fragments of sculpture. The lower tower with the powder magazine, has lately been destroyed by lightning. The remains of antiquity are few and insignificant; part of a Doric frieze and a few small capitals of the Ionic and Corinthian orders, are found in the streets. At the house of the family of Paul may be discovered a curved brick wall, which is called the Odeum. West of the castle, 1,200 yards from the city, on the beach, is the church of Saint Andrea, now a ruin. It has been surrounded with walls, at the angles of which were circular towers. Here the saint was buried, and from this church he is said to have appeared at the battle of Lepanto. At the church of St. Andrea is the Well mentioned by Pausanias as the oracular fountain of Ceres. The Port is about 1,000 yards north of the city, and is scarcely better than an open road, though the anchorage is good. On the shore is a custom-house, with magazines. Of the mountains on the Ætolian side of the gulph, the peaked summit now called Kaki Scala is the ancient Taphiasus and yet emits the fœtid odour noticed by Strabo. To the right, or east, was Macynia, near a spot now marked by a tower. To the left of Taphiasus, on the shore, was Lycorma, or Halicyrna, the ruins of which are yet visible. Calydon was 30 stadia, or 3 miles inland, probably near a place now called Kabro limne. The magnificent mountain of Chalcis, now Galata, suc-ceeds to the west, and beyond it is the mouth of the Evenus, now Phidari, or Ophitari, forming a long and dangerous shoal toward Cape Papa. Beyond this are the salt marshes, or Lake of Mesalongia.

VOSTIZZA TO PATRAS.

H. M.

Quitting the Platanus of Vostizza,

·· 10 A cape runs out to r.

·· 20 A river, or broad torrent.

·· 20 A well l.

·· 3 Cross a river.

·· 37 Cross a bridge. A church l. with tiles and vestiges, perhaps of Rhypæ.

·· 25 More fragments of pottery.

·· 3 Village Longos.

·· 17 Great torrent.

·· 33 A brook. The plain ends. There is another path through the mountains to the left.

·· 7 A khan, prettily situated in a bay at the foot of the chain of Mt. Voidia PANACHAICON. Pretty woods. The khan is called Lampiri.

·· 30 Fountain. A cape r. Beautiful scenery. A church l.

·· 5 A derveni, or guard.

·· 14 A sourie r. below the road.

·· 8 A church r. The road is carried on the side of the mountain. The sea r.

·· 19 Cross a stream.

·· 10 On l. a magnificent water-fall, perhaps 400 feet high.

·· 12 Cross a stream. Fine scenery.

·· 7 Another stream.

·· 5 Having descended to the shore, a lake l. anciently a port, close to which, on a tumulus,
are ancient blocks, possibly a trophy.   The
low promontory of Drepanum, still so called,
commences after passing a second lake, or
ruined port, with a church upon a tumulus r.

·· 60 Opposite to Epacto, or Naupacto, by the Italians called Lepanto.   A tumulus, which is
so large it may be natural, l.   Broken tiles.

·· 63 The coast low.   The castle of the Morea, a
mile distant, r : this is upon the cape anciently called Rhion.

·· 62 Still in a level country.   Having crossed a
river (perhaps the Milichos) where the plain
is about 2 miles wide, the cultivation of Patras begins and the hills called Skata Bouna
approach the road.

·· 25 Patras.

————

8 15

VOSTIZZA TO METOCHI OF MEGASPELIA.

II. M.

At Vostizza, a modern town on the site of the ancient Ægium, is a magnificent platanus on the beach, the trunk of which is 38 feet in circumference and the branches spread 60 feet on each side. There is a copious fountain under it. The anchorage is not safe with a northerly wind. The town is on a flat, to which there is an ascent from the shore, through a subterraneous passage cut in the rock. Here is a mosque, and about 2,000 inhabitants. The houses are not contiguous, but straggling ; and, excepting inconsiderable fragments of the Doric order, contain very few vestiges of antiquity.

·· 35 A great river.

·· 20 A tumulus l.

·· 7 Zeugalathio village, 200 yards r.

·· 17 Cross a mill-stream by a bridge. Sandy point l.

·· 12 Cross river.

·· 34 An orange garden and villa. Myrtles and anemonies. A warm situation, though open to the north. Poplars are in full leaf here in the middle of March.

·· 13 On the hill r. the cave of Hercules. It is accessible by climbing among the bushes.

H.   M.

Before the cave is a terrace wall, and holes in the rock for beams indicate a roof or portico in front. The cavern itself has been much enlarged by art, and a number of niches for votive offerings attest its ancient sanctity.

·· 13 After passing a well l. and leaving the main road l. ascending by a steep road among pines, see l. the foundations of a temple, r. a sepulchral cave.

·· 3 A metochi of Megaspelia—which is 4 hours distant.

———

2 34

MEGASPELIA TO VOSTIZZA.

H. M.

Having descended to the bridge below Megaspelia,

·· 10 Cross another bridge with a pretty mill.

35 After a very steep ascent toward Mt. Phteri,
cross a bridge.

·· 37 On a top, whence is a most magnificent view
of the Gulph of Corinth, with Parnassus,
Helicon, and Pindus beyond—on the side of
Achaia also the country is picturesque and
magnificent.

·· 30 On another summit a most extensive and
beautiful prospect.

·· 35 A fount near a species of isthmus, connecting
the more lofty range of mountains with a
high top covered with the ruins of an ancient
city. This city was Bura, as may be learned
from the cave of Hercules Buraicus on the
north side of the rock. The whole country
exhibits strong marks of the violence of earthquakes.

·· 8 Cross the foundations of 4 walls once securing
the pass between the city and the mountain,
a fountain l. Turn r. under the perpendicular rocks of Bura. L. a picturesque glen,
with a stream running from Mt. Phteri. A
fine fountain said to be among the ruins.

II.	M.	
..	68	Ruined mill l. on the sea-coast. Quit the mountains and cross the river.
..	21	The road quits the bed of a torrent, in which it lies for a considerable distance. The plain on the coast is ill cultivated and about three quarters of a mile wide. The city of Helice, once on the r. of the road, was swallowed up by an earthquake in the 100th olympiad : it contained a magnificent temple of Neptune, whence he was called Heliconiades.
..	25	A village l. distant one mile.
..	10	A mill 500 yards l.
..	10	Village l. and a few dwellings on the shore r.
..	6	A tumulus r.
..	14	A rapid river, sometimes only the bed of a torrent—The Selinus.
..	12	The ruins of a bridge from which the river has strayed.
..	19	Town of Vostizza, on the site of the ancient Ægium.
5	40	

METOCHI OF MEGASPELIA TO ACRATA.

н. м.

·· 5 At the foot of a steep descent among pines turn r. on the bank of the river of Kalabríta, in a most magnificent glen.

·· 10 Cross the river by a bridge and turn l. The chasm through which the stream is precipitated is perhaps one of the most stupendous scenes in the world. The rocks on each side are generally perpendicular, and wherever there is a projection they are fringed with trees and verdure.

·· 12 Turn r. again along the coast, with the sea on l.

·· 17 L. a curious rock shaped by art, with a step, either a tomb, a pedestal, or an altar.

·· 11 Cross a wall. Broken tiles. The sea close on l. The mountain r.

·· 9 Cross a brook.

·· 6 Traces of ancient carriages in the rock, and a cave.

·· 3 Cultivation and a cape l.

·· 12 Cross a river from Diokophto, or Duokopto, a village about one hour distant r.

·· 10 The road lies again on the foot of the hills, with the sea close on l.

·· 5 A cape l.

·· 30 R. a cave and niches.

H. M.

· 6 In a rock r. niches, probably natural.

·· 4 A mill below on l. and source close to the sea.
A low cape l.

·· 14 The khan of Acrata on the bank of a rapid
river. On the mountain above it there is
said to be a palaio kastro, probably near
Diokophto.

---

2 34

ACRATA TO KAMARES.

	Crossing a long bridge over the river Crathis, running from Mt. Crathis. Woody mountains r.
.. 50	Cross a little river. Tiles.
.. 6	A well.
.. 15	Cross a large river, Zaphilitico or Zakoulitico. On the shore tiles and doubtful traces of antiquity. Vines r. Sea l.
.. 39	Rivulet and ruins at Bloubouki. R. is the woody hill on which stood Ægira above the road. L. are the ruins of the port, or Navale Ægiræ, choaked with sand. The black posts upon the two piers have occasioned the name of Mauro Lithari. A derveni.
.. 20	A great Hellenic tomb.
.. 20	Kalybea of Zakoula. A cape l.
.. 2	Mill-stones cut on the road.
.. 2	Cross a river.
.. 55	Tiles.
.. 5	Cross a large stream.
.. 7	A point under the conic hill called Avgò. This is seen from Vostitza. Pretty hills covered with pines.
.. 6	A fountain.
.. 38	Cross a stream.

·· 44 Cross a river in a deep bed from a valley called Gouch.

·· 20 Village of Kamares on the coast l. probably so called from the arches of an aqueduct once standing there. A little farther on the road to Corinth is a khan. On the high peak above Kamares is a church, called the Panagia tes Koruphes. Some have supposed it Gonoessa. The peasants say there are no antiquities on the top, but the prospect must be fine.

———

5 29

KAMARES TO BASILICO.

·· 17 Khan of Kamares, in a plain between the hills
and the coast, with some traces of antiquity,
perhaps the Roman town of Pellene, where
cloth was made.

·· 13 Cross a brook.

·· 45 Cross a large river at Xilo Castro.

·· 20 Well l. The coast sandy.

·· 23 Cross a river.

·· 10 Cross a river.

·· 25 A well-fountain r. A rock close to the road r.
with a wall, and the vestiges of an Ionic
temple of white marble. The columns are
about one foot in diameter. From the ruins
the prospect is fine.

·· 42 A cape r.

·· 15 Cross a river in a ravine.

·· 13 The stones of a Greek water-course.

·· 11 A fluted Doric column, 2 feet 6 inches in
diameter, at Mounzi, a village l. Ascend to
the site of the city of Sicyon.

·· 16 A church built of Hellenic blocks, and the
ruins of a Doric temple.

·· 1 Basilico, a village of 50 houses, situated on
the angle of a little rocky ascent, along which
ran the walls of Sicyon. This city was in
shape triangular, and placed upon a high flat

overlooking the plain, about an hour from
the sea, where is a great tumulus on the
shore. On the highest angle of Sicyon was
the citadel. In the way to it is a Roman
ruin of brick, near which is a theatre and
stadium, of which the masonry is curious.
The situation is magnificent, and was secure
without being inconveniently lofty. Sicyon
was a large city and one of the most ancient
kingdoms of Europe.

4 11

BASILICO TO ALOPEKI.

H. M.

·· 13 Having descended from Basilico, cross a river, over which are two ruined bridges of one arch. The exterior of one is built of large blocks, without cement; the inside is of smaller stones, with mortar.

·· 59 Having turned back, pass under the site of the wall of Sicyon upon the hill r. to the end of the citadel. Cultivation.

·· 30 Ascend by a very steep and crooked path.

4 Cross a stream. A most rugged road.

·· 12 Wall, blocks, and a tower r. Turn r. After this a little cultivation, still ascending. Some vestiges of antiquity. On the summit of the hill r. the site of the temple of Titanos. R. below it, the villages Paradisi and Machini very near together.

·· 60 Village of Alopeki, 30 cottages; whence Corinth bears S. 63 E. The summit where stood the temple is called Agios Elia. The Peribolus and other traces remain. About 30 minutes S. of Alopeki is a ruined Hellenic kastro, small but curious. It is possible this might have been the town of Titanos, and on the summit of the hill a temple. Below this, on a knoll, is a church, with blocks. The place

c

H. M.

much troubled by earthquakes. The view over the Corinthian isthmus and the vale of Agios Giorgios or Phlius is magnificent.

2 58

ALOPEKI TO TRICALA.

H. M.

.. 26 Having ascended a very steep hill, r. is the temple of Titanos. Turning back, a magnificent prospect towards Corinth.

.. 17 A very small plain, with a monastery l. Oaks.

.. 31 Having ascended among oaks, a summit. Descend.

.. 37 Vale and lake of Klementi. The vale seems about 3 miles long. The road crosses it. See Mt. Zyria or Cyllene.

.. 11 Cross a stream running to l. It forms a lake in the plain, whence, by a katabathron, it is said to fall into the lake of Zaracca. See village of Kesra.

.. 19 Ascend from the western side of the plain.

.. 27 Village of Klementi. Chionia, or Kionia, on the lake of Stymphalus, is 2 hours distant.

.. 5 In the village of Klementi a pretty source.

.. 10 A top. Forest of oaks and pines.

.. 6 Road r. to Merkeri.

.. 29 Descend among the most magnificent and beautiful stone pines in the world.

.. 35 A source. Near it a circular stone like an altar half buried.

.. 22 Vale or glen of Tricala opens. The town is seen in 3 divisions, not more than two miles distant in a right line.

H. M.

·· 11 Tiles.

·· 39 Tiles.

·· 10 After a descent, cross a river running from a fine and deep chasm in Zyria l. and falling toward Xylo Kastro. Ascending, turn r.

·· 38 Cross a brook from l. A terrible zigzag ascent.

·· 10 Ruins, of which it is difficult to guess the age. Chapels and trees.

·· 20 Enter Tricala, or Trikkala. The town consists of about 400 houses. The Greek family of Notara, which was formerly of the first dignity, resides here in some degree of splendour and opulence, surrounded by its dependants. The Notaras have also a house at Corinth, where they are not so hospitable as at Tricala. The family still maintains its superiority both in riches and education; and, by retirement to the wintry climate of Mt. Zyria, they live a tolerably independent life. Xylo Kastro is distant about 4 hours, owing to the badness of the road. The situation of Pellene is known to the inhabitants; and colonel Leake visited it below Tricala, upon a rock.

6 43

TRICALA TO ZAKOULA.

H. M

·· 3 Cross a stream.

·· 11 Church of Tricala. Steep zigzag ascent.

·· 41 A summit. Descend. L. an ugly ravine towards Mts. Zyria and Chelmos. Cultivated,
but ugly country.

·· 63 Karia, a village consisting of 120 houses.
Many walnut-trees. A river runs to l. toward
Phonia. Very high situation.

·· 34 Cross a stream running to the Phonia river.
Enter a valley. Road l. to Kalabrita, Klouchines, and Sarandapico, a village half an
hour distant; also to Agia Barbara, distant
three hours. To Klouchines, consisting of
several villages, (near one of which is the
Styx, in Mount Chelmos) and Nonacris, the
peasants call one hour. From Klouchines
to Kalabrita, 5 hours.

·· 18 Descend among fine firs, of the species called
Peukos.

·· 42 A long descent in a valley. High wooded
rocks r. The dry bed of the river makes a
good road. A fine source. A second stream
Sopoto falls in. Descend by a very steep
road.

·· 56 Village of Zakoula in several portions,

―――――

4 28

ZAKOULA TO ACRATA.

H.	M.	
2	2	Pass through a chasm in the mountain l. At the top of the pass r. is a precipitous rock, on which it is possible the castle of Phelloe might have been situated. Quit the valley of Zakoula. Descend, among beautiful pines on magnificent mountains, to the sea-coast between Acrata and Kamares. Turn l.
1	48	Having proceeded along the road from Kamares, reach the khan of Acrata.
3	50	

PATRA TO PALAIO ACHAIA.

H. M.

.. 6 On the shore, by the church of St. Andrea
and well of Ceres.

.. 4 Cross a water-course.

.. 6 Cross a river from Mt. Boidia. Vines and
olives l.

.. 9 Having crossed 2 streams, a cape r.

.. 5 Two artificial canals.

.. 8 Two artificial canals. Saravalle village l. on
a mountain. Another stream.

.. 4 A bridge l. Stream and marshes.

.. 5 Bridge l. Fine river Leuka—GLAUCUS.

.. 11 Two capes r.

.. 17 Cross a river. Cape r.

.. 3 Neochorio three-quarters of a mile l. Coast
turns towards the west.

.. 7 Platanus and fount l. Plain three-quarters
of a mile wide.

.. 10 Cross stream at point of an insulated hill.

.. 21 Cross a torrent bed, and fount l. Fields.

.. 5 Ruined brick aqueduct.

.. 16 Ruined brick aqueduct.

.. 6 Stones and ruins.

.. 2 Cross 2 walls. Tiles.

.. 34 Well l. Sea close r.

.. 31 Vale, after a plain.

.. 2 Banks of the Raminitza, a deep river and very

H. M.

difficult ford.   At least 14 minutes are employed in crossing it with baggage.   On the
l. among the trees are the ruins of a city—
Olenus.   R. marshes.   A few huts.

.. 23   Khan with inscriptions.   The ruins are about
200 yards south of it.   On the shore a custom-house.   The ruins consist of the foundations of the city walls placed on the top of a
natural bank, now shaded by oaks.

3   55

PALAIO ACHAIA TO METOKI.

II. M.

·· 10   Cross a brook and turn l. Road to Gas-
        tugni l.
·· 10   Road to Kalybea of Gerbash, a village on the
        mountain l.
·· 25   Cross a wall.   Herds of wild swine.
·· 3   Tumulus and stones l.
·· 4   Kalybea 500 yards r.   A pool l.
·· 8   A church r.   Gomasto village one hour and a
        quarter distant to the left.
·· 10   Vestiges l. called Palaio Kastro.   Stones in
        lines.   The city of Dyme.
·· 15   Vestiges.
·· 15   Huts and well l.   Forests of Velanea oak.
·· 7   Karabosta village.   Tombs and vases found
        here.
·· 5   Church and fount.
·· 2   Cross a river.
·· 10   A church.
·· 7   Limne, or lake, extending to Cape Papa r.
        Many fish caught here.
·· 18   Having left a church r. a kastro upon a
        rocky hill.   The walls ill built, and without
        towers.
·· 28   Cross a river running to a marsh r.   Oaks.   A
        metoki r.   The river Larisos to the left.

H. M.

.. 25 Turning r. the metoki, where strangers may
       lodge.
——————
3 22

ELIS.

		H.	M.	Computed Miles.
14.	Метосни to Kapelletti	3	25	. . . 6
15.	Kapelletti to Palaiopoli	5	14	. . . 10
16.	Palaiopoli to Pyrgo	6	18	. . . 15
17.	Pyrgo to Phloka	3	23	. . . 8
18.	Phloka to Olympia and Palaio Phanaro	2	17	. . . 7
19.	Palaio Phanaro to Brina	4	7	. . . 10
20.	Brina to Agios Isidoro	3	30	. . . 8
21.	Agios Isidoro to Strovitzi . . .	3	11	. . . 8
22.	Agios Isidoro to Arcadia . . .	5	41	. . . 15

METOCHI TO CAPELLETTI.

H. M.

Pass through a forest of oaks, abounding in wild hogs, of the antique form. Turning r. by a tumulus, and stones l. proceed in a direction nearly west. The soil is sandy.

·· 80 Tou Ali Chelibey village, the country-house, or pyrgo, of a Turk.

A road r. to Konopeli, a rock on the coast, with a little sandy bay. On the beach is a mineral spring. On the summit are the vestiges of an ancient fortress. The place bears N. 43 W. from the village of Ali Chelibey. Cross a river. R. is a lake.

·· 25 Cross a river. Road runs SW. Many oaks and myrtles.

·· 15 Cross a river.

·· 15 Monoladi metochi and church r. 1 mile. Cross 2 bridges.

·· 8 Cross a river.

·· 4 Fount r.

·· 28 Cross a stream, running to a great lake r. on the coast, with a woody cape. Sandy shore.

·· 7 Turn l. quitting the main road. Tiles.

·· 23 Capelletti, 3 houses in a great wood. From

H.　M.

Capelletti, Portes, probably the Pylos of Elis, is 5 hours distant, under a mountain called Mauro Bouné.

3　25

KAPELLETTI TO PALAIOPOLIS.

H. M.

.. 10 Cross a brook. Woods.

.. 14 Kaloteichos village r.

.. 6 L. a church, and tumulus, and small column. Vestiges of high antiquity. Buprasium in this part of Elis. See village of Eratouni r. in a line with Chlomouki, or Castel Tornese. R. see Lechiana. Turn l. having gone W. Country becomes less woody.

.. 22 Cross a brook.

.. 23 Cross a bridge. L. a kalybea of Mazi, a village near Phanaro, 12 hours distant. L. of Chlomouki a village. Teke. R. Kastri, and a monastery Blakeriana. A fountain l.

.. 24 Cross a river. Perhaps the Larissus of Pausanias.

.. 54 Having passed on r. the direct road to Castagni, and descended among the half-buried remains of great earthenware wine-vessels to a wet plain, cross a river. A church l. and tumulus.

.. 19 A bushy plain, where the Turks course hares. A tumulus r.

.. 23 Cross a river. Three tumuli l. R. of Castel Tornese see Neochori. R. Andravida.

.. 6 Lechiana 1 hour r. Chelebey l. Brate 2 miles r.

H.	M.	
•	4	Cross a river. A tumulus r.
••	15	Tragano, or Dragano. Turn l. A church r.
••	9	Village of Agios Sosti.
••	21	Ford of the Peneus, a broad and rapid river.
••	30	Village r. half a mile.
••	12	Kalybea in the plain.
••	4	Roman ruin, on the site of a part of the city of Elis.
••	18	Village of Palaiopolis. The tower above is called Kaloscopi, or Belvedere.

—————

5 14

PALAIOPOLI (ELIS) TO PYRGO.

H.	M.	
..	5	Brook in the plain.
..	15	At foot of the eminences bounding the plain.
..	7	A church and tumuli. A village l.
..	16	Tumulus r. Tiles.
..	4	Cross a stream. Sand hillocks r.
..	6	Having crossed a stream, a village r. quarter of a mile.
..	5	Castugni seen r.
..	42	Village Koki l.
..	6	Cross a river, with deep banks.
..	49	Cross a river. Village Dervitzi Chelibey.
..	15	Tumulus, and stones, l.
..	13	Village r. Another l.
..	4	Cross a river. Another village r.
..	18	A little hollow. Cross a stream.
..	10	Cross a little river.
..	7	Mesalongachi village, one mile and a half from the sea.
..	28	Katacolo Kastro r. 1 mile.
..	23	Tiles, having descended into another plain, and turned a little l.
..	42	Cross a water-course.
..	51	Cross a bridge.
..	13	Village of Pyrgo. Here is a hospitable bishop, styled of Olonos and Pylos. The

D

town is under the government of the agas of Lalla, who are the real sovereigns of the country. The Lalliotes are an Albanian tribe of Mahometans, and have taken possession of the district by force. The town is situated on a high plain, between Mt. Olonos and the Alpheus. They have a bad character among the Greeks, but seem brave and hospitable.

6 19

PYRGO TO PHLOKA.

.. 26 Blocks l. Proceed up the valley of the Alpheus on its right bank.

.. 7 Hill, and tiles, l.

.. 50 Knoll, and caves, l. The road ascends the projection of a hill.

.. 14 Descend

.. 3 A large plain. Coccoura village l. a quarter of a mile. Boulantza r. on the opposite bank of Alpheus. The l. bank of the river prettily wooded. Strephi l.

.. 20 A marshy plain.

.. 26 See r. over the river Bourkir, a country-house, very pleasantly situated. Above it, in the distance, observe the peak called Phanario, on Mt. Smyrne.

.. 51 A church r. with a fluted Doric column, about 18 inches in diameter.

.. 6 Pretty village of Phloka. The inhabitants, who are all Turks, are very civil to strangers. They are chiefly apostate Christians, and some of them preserve their original names, as Mustapha Johannes, Ali Anastasio, &c. Antilalla, or OLYMPIA, is about 35 minutes distant.

3 23

PHLOKA TO PALAIO PHANARO.

H. M.

Ascend from Phloka. Rough ground.

·· 23 A valley, with the Cladeus flowing from l. Antilalla, anciently OLYMPIA.

·· 12 Cross the Cladeus, in a deep bed, a mill. A Roman ruin near, of brick. A road l. up the glen to Lalla. See the village Rasi, on the other side of the Alpheus. Having passed the Cladeus, turn r. Mt. of Saturn l. having passed which, turn l. again. At the point of the hill is a tumulus r. The ruins of the temple of Jupiter are 55 geographic paces distant from the hill, toward the Alpheus. There are several bushes which mark the spot, and the Turks of Lalla are often employed in excavating the stones. Between the temple and the river, in the descent of the bank, are vestiges of the Hippodrome, or buildings serving for the celebration of the Olympic games. These accompany the road to Miracca on the r. to some distance. L. pretty hills, with wood. The whole valley very beautiful.

·· 30 After passing a stream from l. and a spot where are several ancient sepulchres r. ascend to Miracca, a little Turkish village, where an aga of Lalla has a very convenient pyrgo, built of the stone of the temple. In the village are kept many large and ferocious dogs. Earthquakes are here frequent.

·· 27 Descend from Miracca, which is situated on a point projecting into the valley. Cross a river, before which fragments of tiles. A kalybea l. on the hill.

·· 15 The ferry of Palaio Phanaro. Horses swim over, and passengers are carried in a monoxylos, the hollow trunk of a platanus, one by one. Nine horses, and baggage, employ sometimes 2 hours in the passage.

·· 30 Hence a most dangerous path ascends, among pines, to the village of Palaio Phanaro, where are 25 houses, and the tower, or pyrgo, of Ali Aga, a hospitable Turk of Lalla. On the ascent is a fount. The loaded horses, unable to avoid the trees, frequently fall down the declivity toward the river, till arrested by other trees. From the summit of the conic mount of Palaio Phanaro, is a beautiful view, in each direction, toward Elis and Arcadia, of the course of the river. Slight indications of an ancient town, or fortress, may be discerned.

2 17

PALAIO PHANARO TO BRINA.

H. M.

.. 7 After a steep descent to the left bank of the Alpheus, turn r. See Kutchukeri.

.. 13 Turn more r.

.. 20 Cross a stream.

.. 5 Kutchukeri r. across the valley, distant about a mile.

.. 35 The road, where any exists, very bad, but the country is pretty and woody.

.. 21 The peak on Mt. Smyrne, or Minthe, l. On the summit the natives say there was a fortress.

.. 10 Mundritza, a very pretty village, a mile l. Sandy hills, and pine woods.

.. 25 Cross the Mundritza river.

.. 15 Recross the river.

.. 8 Tiles.

.. 30 Chrystina village r. 200 yards. Cross a brook. Turn l.

.. 35 Leaving Risavo r. ascend the woody hill of Brina, a small village.

.. 23 Brina. The peaked summit, said to be a palaio kastro, is near Brina. Fruit trees blossom here in January.

4 7

BRINA TO AGIO ISIDORO.

н. м.

·· 14 In a valley below Brina.   Pine woods.
·· 10 Ascend.
·· 7   Fount r.
·· 10 Descent among firs.
·· 5   See the sea, and a lake on the coast formed
       by a narrow bank of sand covered with
       pines.
·· 19 Cross to l. bank of a stream, to the village
       Alona.
·· 11 Tiles, evidently fallen from a fortress above.
·· 7   A church r.   See Agolinitza r.   Fount and
       platanus.   Turn l.
·· 28 A mound or tumulus r.   A palaio kastro on
       the rock l.   The walls and towers are in good
       preservation.   SAMICON.
·· 7   Derveni of Kleidi (the key of the pass), be-
       tweeen Mt. Smyrne, or Minthe, and the sea.
       A fishery in the lake, though it be the reci-
       pient of the waters of the Anigrus.   The der-
       veni is a ruin.
·· 26 Turn r.   The sea r.   A lake l.   Sandy hills
       with pools.   Beautiful pines.
·· 21 Lake ends l.   A road runs l. to Xerro Chorio.
·· 45 Khan of Agio Isidoro, pronounced Ayo Si-
       dero, a melancholy spot nearly deserted.   A
       river from Chrysouli, a kastro on Mt. Albena,

falls into the sea S. of the khan. About 2 miles inland is Palaio Biskini, or Pischini, probably PYLOS TRIPHYLIACUS. Near this is a village called Sarene—εις Αργηνην. Hence to Sidero Kastro, 5 hours. To Graditza, 6 hours.

3 30

AGIO ISIDORO TO STROVITZI.

H. M.

Cross the river behind the khan.

·· 41 Cross a bridge over a brook.

·· 14 A well l. and a kalybea, of Glatza distant a quarter of a mile. L. little hills near the road, which is on a sandy coast, with many pines.

·· 47 Near a tower l. quit the coast, and turn l. up a pretty woody glen with a river.

·· 16 A kalybea l.

·· 5 A kalybea; after which, a range of stones. The place is strewed with tiles or pottery. Above is a little cave in a sandy rock, with many niches, as if for votive offerings.

·· 22 The glen contracts. Cross a brook from l. In the rock l. a hollow.

·· 8 Stones and a ruined church r.

·· 3 A mill, turned by a great stream from a fine fount l.

·· 28 Ascend by a steep path. Waterfalls and Platani. A high peak r. Several mills.

·· 7 Village and orange-trees, Strobitzi, or Strovitzi. From the village there is a very steep ascent, once strongly fortified, to a flat summit or table hill. A curious gate remains, probably Lepreon or LEPREUM. From the

H. M.

fortress Paulitza is seen and Mt. Tetrage;
also the valley of the Neda. On the north-
east is Mofkitza, where is a palaio kastro,
possibly MACISTUS.

3   11

KHAN OF AGIO ISIDORO TO ARCADIA.

п. м.

The road lies all on the coast. (Vid. route to Strobitzi.

·· 41 Bridge.

·· 14 Well and kalybea of Glatza.

·· 47 Near a tower, road l. to Strovitzi. Cross a river. L. vestiges, or foundations.

·· 10 Ruins on hill l.

·· 15 Blocks of stone and marble, with tiles.

·· 5 Marsh r. The valley of the Neda l. L. the villages Upana and Kato Elea.

·· 15 The bridge of Bouzi, or Neda, and the khan on l. bank.

·· 10 Chilia Modia, a few stones so called.

·· 15 Fountain l. Above, on l. is Argaliana.

·· 8 Kleidi r. on an insulated knoll, where was a derveni.

·· 1 Steno, a rock. The people say there is an inscription upon it.

·· 15 Fountain, stream, and blocks of stone.

·· 28 Sandanoi. L. a conical hill, of a red colour, terminating the pass between the hills of Triphilia and the sea. A vale opens on l.

·· 7 Eminences terminate on l.

·· 35 Cross a bridge of 5 arches. Forest of olives.

·· 75 City of Arcadia.

5 41

MESSENIA.

	H. M.	Computed Miles.
23. PHILIATRA to Arcadia	2 50	. . . 8
24. Gargagliano to Philiatra	2 55	. . . 8
25. Navarino to Gargagliano . . .	5 15	. . .10
26. Neocastro to Mothone	2 0	. . . 7
27. Arcadia to Kleissoura	4 21	. . .12
28. Kleissoura to Constantino . . .	3 0	. . . 6
29. Konstantino to Mavromati . . .	4 23	. . .10
30. Mavromati to Khan of Sakona . .	4 5	. . .10
31. Sakona Khan to Scala	1 41	. . . 5
32. Scala to Calamata	4 6	. . .12
33. Calamata to Chytries	3 34	. . . 8
34. Khan of Sakona to Krano . ; .	2 42	. . . 6
35. Arcadia to Sidero Kastro . . .	3 40	. . . 8
36. Sidero Kastro to Paulitza . . .	4 0	. . . 9
37. Leondari to Khan of Sakona, by Makryplai	3 29	. . . 8

PHILIATRA TO ARCADIA.

· 24 Quitting the grove and village of Philiatra, the hills cease on r. and a more distant branch is seen in the same direction.

·· 8 A valley, with a river, Philiatro Nerro.

·· 2 Cross the bridge. See below on l. ruins of two others. R. the village Kanaloupou, or Khanalopou, and near it another, called Chalaizone. The great mountain r. is called Alia, probably Agios Elias. The sea one mile l. A shrubby plain of red sand and clay. The more distant hill r. is called Geranion. L. near the coast, Katochalaizone. Balaclava village r.

·· 26 Bridge of the river Balaklava in a glen.

·· 3 Another branch of the same. Cross the road from Balaclava to Katochalaizone. Ascend. A village, Arminiou; and, higher on, Mt. Mallia, or Mali Agiani.

·· 34 A villa L. Sea half a mile l.

·· 6 Mt. Mali approaches on r.

·· 12 A fountain r.

·· 5 A running brook and villa r.

·· 13 L. A church of Agios Giorgios. Wood of olives.

·· 7 A little bridge.

·· 5 R. huts.

H. M.

·· 12 Rivulet, with a little bridge and a clear fount.
       A ruined wall.
·· 3 Ascend to Arcadia.
·· 10 Passing 2 ruined chapels, enter the town of
       Arcadia. The citadel is probably on the
       site of the castle of Cyparissia, the fort is
       now decayed, and the town becoming ruinous.
       It has no port; below, in the way to the sea,
       are some Doric fragments of marble, and in
       the city are some Turkish baths. The whole
       country is a fine grove of olives, the moun-
       tains rising close above the town.

2 50

GARGAGLIANO TO PHILIATRA.

·· 3 A fount and well on the descent from Gargagliano to the plain.

·· 15 A road to the coast opposite the Isle of Prote, called by the Italians Prodano, l. Caves r. in the rocks.

·· 20 A cave r. in the foot of the hill, producing nitre. Barutou Spelia. Velania oaks.

·· 11 R. village of Balta, distant 30 minutes, and Morena distant one hour.

· 4 Kutchuveri, a wooded knoll, l.

·· 10 In a glen r. a cave called Cochino Patera.

·· 5 L. on the coast, the ruins of Ordina, or Ortina.

·· 7 Over a shrubby plain to the river Longobardo, descend to it. L. a fountain, and bridge. Ascending from the river, myrtles and wild lupins.

·· 51 Descend to a river, and a fountain called Agian Kyriaki, running to the port of Philiatra.

·· 21 Olive grove.

·· 28 Fine oak l. under which a chapel of St. John. R. a church of S. Nicolo. The plain is broad, and well cultivated. The village of Philiatra is large, and has a new mosque.

E

H. M.

The houses are scattered, and there is a fine cypress among the olives.   Here are several vineyards.   The Mainiote pirates sometimes land at this place to plunder.

2 55

NAVARINO, OR NEOKASTRO, TO GARGAGLIANO.

H. M.
·· 27 Having proceeded by a bad road from the fountain in the Greek village of Navarino, l. a ruined tower, r. a fountain. The port l.

·· 10 In the plain.

·· 3 A ruined bridge, and little river.

·· 2 Another stream.

·· 3 Ascend.

·· 3 A plain. Mt. Tabolachi, or Pilaw, r. a conic hill.

·· 9 A ruined bridge, with deep water. Beshli. Two small brooks, and one after. R. a pretty glen.

·· 1 A bridge, and rice field, in a marshy plain.

·· 12 The hills from r. approach the water. Rice grounds and shrubby hills.

·· 8 A river. On r. bank a garden. Turn NE. Church of Agio Nicolo r.

·· 7 River Kourbeh.

·· 5 The bridge.

·· 10 Hills close to the road on r. Under the rock of old Navarino, or Pylos, is a white house, and l. of it the village Petrachorio.

·· 20 Boidochilia, at the north end of Pylos, l. A hut or place called Geophyre, perhaps a bridge. A grove of olives.

·· 19 An eminence approaches the road r. The

E 2

H. M.

plain extends on r. See the villages, or tchifliks of Osman Aga and Haslan Aga.

·· 4   A platanus and aqueduct.

·· 2   A well, house, and hill called Lirachi.

·· 19   R. a wooded valley, and bridge over the Romanos.

·· 19   On the top of the opposite bank.

·· 18   Descend. Heath and trees.

·· 7   A water-course. Wild rocks and trees r. and l.

·· 2   Brisomero Nerro, and a woody dell.

·· 12   A water-course, or aqueduct. Arbutus.

·· 28   A summit, after a steep and dangerous descent.

· 7   A cultivated hollow.

·· 18   A semicircular valley.

·· 23   A summit.

· 5   See Gargagliano.

·· 9   Chapel of St. Nicholo.

·· 3   Gargagliano, a large Greek village overlooking a plain, and Prote to the west. The houses are good, and the situation, which is lofty, is much embellished by many cypresses.

5   15

NEOKASTRO TO MOTHONE.

H. M.

·· 13 Pass a little bridge over a ravine, after an ascent from the lower Greek village of Navarino. The fort of Neokastro r. and Mt. St. Nicolo.

·· 12 Cross the ravine. The road to Corone r. An ascent between two mountains. Very bad road, sometimes paved, by an aqueduct. L. several caves high among the rocks.

·· 11 L. a wood of cypresses and mulberries. Cultivation on terraces. The ancient road very perfect, consisting of small stones very well united, not more than 6 feet broad—perhaps Venetian. On the top of the pass, Navarino bears N. by W. and Mothone S. by W.

·· 9 Descending, in the rock l. caves.

·· 10 Enter a plain by a lime-kiln.

·· 4 Olives.

·· 6 L. on an eminence, the village Opshinò.

·· 5 Other houses of Opshinò.

·· 2 An old olive-tree, called Agyria, and said to be half-way between Navarino and Modon.

·· 8 A peribolia and villa l. More distant, see the village Dia ta Bathenai. L. the village Metaxadi.

·· 10 Agio Nicolo Mt. approaches the road.

·· 2 Ruined chapel l. in a marshy spot.

·· 5 Below Metaxadi, a tchiftlik keupritchu kevi.
R. a cave, with something like holes for vo-
tive offerings. Below it an ancient quarry.
L. a ruined church.

·· 5 Ruined foundations.

·· 3 Agatchu, a Turkish village, l. Beyond it a
villa.

·· 5 In a hollow, r. a corn-mill, l. a quarry.

·· 3 L. across a stream, a peribolia.

·· 7 Greek village of Mothone, or Modon, with a
pretty kiosk and garden of the Bey l. E. of
Modon, about 2700 paces from the city, is a
place called Palaio Mothone, where are the
vestiges of a city, with a citadel, and a few
marbles. It is difficult to determine the date
of the ruins. A river runs half round it. The
fortress of Modon is Venetian, and is entered
by a bridge. There is an aga of the janis-
saries here, and a little port; but ships often
anchor at the opposite island of Sapienza.
The plain E. of Modon is fertile, and abounds
in olives. In the Greek town live several
vice-consuls of foreign nations. The Turkish town is falling to decay. Modon is
about 7 miles from Neocastro.

_____

2 0

ARCADIA TO KLEISSOURA.

II.　M.

Quitting the castle of Arcadia, the road lies under fine olive trees.

·· 16 The great mountain r. retires.

·· 3 Memilliáno village r. on hill foot. Ascend.

·· 47 Sandanoi, or Sandaboi, the entrance into Triphylia l.

·· 3 A top. Descend.

·· 24 Cross a stream from r. after a steep descent, and immediately after, the Arcadia river. R. a rocky summit with vestiges. Turn a little r.

·· 17 A bridge over a ravine. Bad road.

·· 8 Sidero Kastro seen on l. Alimachi village seen high up the hill r. See Mt. Psichro, on south side of which is a village, Lendeka. A fountain which cures all maladies or kills the patient.

·· 11 Stream and ravine of Kakorema, where sometimes robbers are stationed.

·· 37 An anathema.

·· 10 Ruins and tiles. Mountains from l. near the road. A village seen l.

·· 8 A church r.

·· 2 Cross a stream from l.

·· 10 A conic hill l. with castle of Lapi and village.

H. M.

·· 30 Cross a river from l.   Turn l. from main road
to Tripolitza.

·· 25 A marshy plain, in which run many branches
of a river in artificial canals.

·· 10 After passing three other branches, the village and pyrgo of Kleissoura.   Kleissoura
is a little village, with vestiges of antiquity,
under the south side of Mt. Tetrasi, Tetrage,
or Tetrazi. Cerausios. There is a path from
Kleissoura over the mountain to Kacoletri,
where is a palaio kastro, in some respects
corresponding to Ira, and near the temple of
Apollo at Bassæ.   On a hill near Kleissoura
are some ruins.

---

4 21

KLEISSOURA TO KONSTANTINO.

H. M.

·· 43   Having descended from Kleissoura, the rapid river of Kokla, which runs with the Mauro Zume into the Gulph of Coron. Turn sharp l. in joining the road to Tripolitza.

·· 47   Open groves of oak. L. across the river, on a high insulated eminence, is a palaio kastro. The ruins are fine modern towers, perhaps on old foundations. Having passed a ravine, and arrived at the village of Aliture in the Stenyclerian plain, turn l. out of the main road, and

·· 68   See the village of Booza, or Bouga.

·· 19   An eminence and kastro r. Ascend.

·· S   Village of Konstantino. A large village, well armed against the thieves, who often infest the country. There is another path to Kleissoura, over the foot of Tetrazi. In the plain or pass to the north is a place or knoll called Gerana with the appearance of a kastro. Two places in Messenia bore names like this, Carnion and Karnessia.

3   0

KONSTANTINO TO MAVROMMATI.

H. M.

·· 27 Having descended to south from Konstantino, cross a brook from r.

·· 32 Village of Alitouri, and r. the opening of the valley towards Arcadia.

·· 26 The ruins of a most singular ancient bridge resting on piers in the centre, at the junction of two rivers, whence arches, in three different directions, lead to the three points of land formed by the confluence. It is what is called a triangular bridge in a similar case at Crowland in Lincolnshire. The ancient bridge seems to have been constructed with approaching blocks, not an arch; so that the bridge may be of considerable antiquity. Two piers remain above water, and one to a considerable height.

·· 50 Koleni village r. on the foot of Mount Vourkano, or Ithome.

·· 23 R. having proceeded in a pretty country, is the gap between the two tops of Mt. Vourkano Ithome and Evan. Cross a brook, and turn r. up a steep ascent.

·· 65 Monastery and cypresses in a beautiful and lofty situation on Mount Ithome. In the walls, two beautiful feet of a white marble statue.

H. M.

·· 20 Having climbed still higher, reach the pass between Mts. Evan l. and Ithome r. and pass the walls of the city of Messene. A fine view.

·· 20 After a long descent, Mavrommati, a small village, with a beautiful source, under Ithome, in the centre of the ancient city.

4 23

MAVROMMATI TO KHAN OF SAKONA.

H. M.

Quitting the fount of Mavrommati, see l. when the road turns north, a marble basin, and a hollow like a naumachium. Mt. Ithome r.

.. 27 Gate of Messene. The architrave, 19 feet long, lies at the inner gate, which opens into a circular court, 62 feet in diameter. The outer gate was between two towers, 33 feet asunder. The whole is of beautiful and magnificent blocks, as are all the walls, and of the age of Epaminondas. Under a niche on r. in the circular court, is a defaced inscription, relating to a statue placed there, perhaps, in Roman times. The walls run up Mt. Ithome r. and are in fine preservation, enclosing a vast extent of ground. The inner gates had a division forming a small passage for persons on foot, and a road for carriages.

. 33 Having passed some tombs, descend along the north side of Ithome, among trees, keeping in front the old Venetian castle of Mylæ.

.. 15 Besh, a village, on the foot of Mt. Ithome.

.. 20 L. a church, and a tumulus with a block lying near it.

.. 15 Cross a stream.

H. M.

·· 10 Cross the triangular bridge. It is, perhaps, of the time of Epaminondas.

·· 20 Zeza village r. Cross a stream.

·· 25 Melegala l. The Stenyclerian plain.

·· 13 Cross the road to Scala on r.

·· 67 Khan of Sakona, at the foot of Macryplai.

4 5

KHAN OF SAKONA TO SCALA.

.. 17 Proceeding southward along the plain anciently called Stenyclerian, cross a stream from l.

.. 3 L. the vestiges of a city wall. The city must have been on the side of the hill.

.. 3 Cross another stream from l. The mountains l. are the projections from the branches of Taygetus.

.. 11 A farm-house r. See r. across the plain several towers on a hill. It is called a palaio kastro, but the ruin is of modern construction : the guides called it Mylæ. The plain is marshy, but produces much Indian corn. A church on l.

.. 22 Cross a brook from l. A church ruined r.

.. 3 Ruin r. and a derveni. See r. Mele Gala, a village, on an eminence in the plain. L. is an insulated mount or rock, with a church upon it, and below the church a cave. Beyond it Mt. Bala, or Pala, bounds the plain l.

.. 12 Hills on l. with some vestiges near. Cross a brook. The country covered with wild lavender.

.. 23 Having ascended, and turned a little l. observe the strata of the rocks, like a natural mosaic

H.   M.

pavement, on a knoll. Descending see Scala
and the sea.

·· 7 Scala, a village, on a knoll, part of a range of
eminences dividing the plains of Stenyclerus
and the Pamisus, and extending from Mt.
Ithome, now Vourkano, to the branches of
Taygetus, Scala has several gardens, protected by hedges of prickly Indian figs.

———
1   41

SCALA TO CALAMATA.

- ·· 17 Having descended into the plain south of Scala, find a stream r. L. a tumulus.
- ·· 8 A marsh and mill r.
- ·· 5 A glen.
- ·· 3 Foundation of a small temple, below which is a rock and fountain, and a pool produced by it. Source of the river Pamisus, where infants were purified.
- ·· 1 A lime-kiln, and another similar rock and pool.
- ·· 6 Having hitherto skirted the plain, enter the flattest part of it. A very fine source r. Many buffaloes in the marsh. See r. the town of Giafaramini.
- ·· 3 A magnificent source, forming a river, r. Branch of Pamisus. Fine trees at the source, which has been walled round. L. a chapel of Agios Giorgios. R. a derveni.
- ·· 2 R. the plain, cultivated: beyond is the great marsh. The road is perfectly fine.
- ·· 36 Village near on r. Gaidaro Chorio, surrounded by Indian figs. L. village of Pedimo, at the foot of the hill. A fount there.
- ·· 9 Turn l. over a bridge. River runs to r. R. village of Brakati. Fig and mulberry trees. Caves on the hill l.

II. M.

·· 12 L. is a place called Palaio Castro (Thuria). Poplars on the road.

·· 8 Two miles r. Haslan Aga's village, and cypresses. R. at a distance, the town of Nisi. L. Ais Aga, and further on, Karnichi.

·· 5 Loutro. A large Roman ruined bath of brick. Aqueducts and pipes remain. Fig trees and mulberries. Marsh r.

·· 7 An old church l. Another also l.

·· 7 High hedges of prickly figs almost meet over the road.

·· 15 Village Delli Hassan l. The road turns a little l.

·· 1 A khan l. Tombs r. Crossing a river these tombs are on l. Olives.

·· 11 Ruined church l. Another r.

·· 8 Kulchanoe l. A road runs to it. Fields and hedges.

· 10 Ais Aga village l. Cypresses and a village r. Excellent road.

·· 5 A peribolia and villa l. See Nisi r.

·· 5 The appearance of modern fortifications.

·· 10 A river r. A tower l. on the hill, and village r. of it.

·· 7 Village of Asprochomo. Sand hills.

·· 13 A chapel l. Olives. Hills about half a mile l. Red soil. On mount l. monastery Agios Gas. Another in front.

·· 10 Descending into a hollow. Olives. Mulberries and mastic.

F

H. M.

·· 14 L. in a hollow, a chapel.
·· 14 Enter Kalamata, crossing a river. Fine orange
      and lemon gardens.   Good houses.

4 12

CALAMATA TO CHYTRIES.

п. м.

·· 13 A stream flowing among fields and olive groves.

·· 5 A tower l. and another r. Fountain l.

·· 4 A brook. Road turns from south-east to south.

·· 2 A brook. Fig trees. A church and houses r.

·· 7 A river.

·· 6 R. a pyrgo of the Bey of Maina. The isle Venetico seen behind Coron. Mt. Jenitza l.

·· 5 Crossing a river, enter the territory of Maina. Maina is a country which includes Mt. Taygetus and many of its branches. This country has never entirely submitted to the Turks.

·· 10 In a little hollow a church. The angle of the gulf. The sea close on r. Many corn fields l. below Jenitza.

·· 20 A hollow. Fields of chamomile and lupins.

·· 5 Kalithea Chorio l. one mile distant. Cross the bed of a torrent.

·· 6 A new church, 200 yards distant l.

·· 6 A salt and purgative source r.

·· 5 Pass a ravine, and a wall, built by the Mainiotes to repel the Turks. A circular tower l. and a new square tower r. The place called Almiro. Salt water.

·· 17 Bed of a torrent. Olives r.

·· 4 A deep hollow, with mulberry trees.

P 2

••	5	A furious stream, rushing out of a cavern and turning a mill. The stream is said to be augmented by a south-east wind, and the natives think it comes from the sea at Marathonisi.
••	4	Cypresses, and a manufactory of tiles.
••	3	The road runs under a rock on the beach.
••	2	Medenia, a village, l. 2 miles.
••	23	Having passed 2 little capes, Palaio Chora, now only a church, with a Romaic inscription. Ships water here. Many wells. See
•		the snowy peaks of Taygetus, or St. Elea. Some tiles show that a town once stood here.
••	4	Having passed a church l. a glen
••	3	A well, and dangerous rocky descent. A tile manufactory in a bay.
••	10	Descend from a high rock. Caves r. Church r. and l.
•	9	Glen, with a stream from Taygetus.
••	4	A sandy beach. Rock l.
••	3	A pass between a rock and the sea.
••	21	A bay, with a stream.
••	8	Chytries, a castle of the Bey of Maina.

3 34

KHAN OF SAKONA TO KRANO.

H. M.

·· 12 Three churches. Quit the plain.

·· 6 Village called Philia. Mosque and steep hill.

·· 32 Cross the road from Arcadia to Lontari. Forest of oaks.

·· 8 R. across a glen and river, on a hill formed by the foot of Mount Tetrage, are ruins called Sandani (Andania).

·· 11 Kalybea of Krano. Tiles.

·· 23 Wall. The city Carnasium was in this part of the country.

·· 5 Cross another wall.

·· 27 Stream, with a fall. A rocky ridge turns the path to the left. Here are tiles at a steep hill.

·· 30 Krano l. at which arrive after

·· 8 Crossing a stream and an ascent. Krano·is a village, with a derveni or guard, situated on the ridge extending from Mt. Taygetus to Mt. Lycæus: from above the village there is an extensive view of the plains of Megalopolis and Messenia. The summit of Mt. Ithome bears 5 47 W.

ARCADIA TO SIDERO KASTRO, OR ISIDORO KASTRO.

H. M.

.. 5 Quitting Arcadia, anciently CIPARISSIA, cross a stream.

.. 10 Olives and corn. Xero Brisse, a fountain, dry in summer.

.. 2 A stream, Cartela.

.. 8 See l. of Brisse another village, Daoud Aga. R. of these is Belemina, a ·small village, above which is a monastery, called Katsemi‑kada.

.. 4 Cross a brook, shaded by thickets of cistus. Quit the olive grove. The mountain of Arcadia ends on r.

.. 25 A river, with a bridge toward the sea, l.

.. 10 On a summit a church l.

- 31 Arcadia river, ascending from which see ·r. Alimaki and l. Marmara. Vestiges near the ford.

.. 30 A rivulet, and road to Marmara.

.. 20 Village of Kakavo r.

.. 12 Rivulet. The country is covered with oaks, arbutus, myrtles, and salvia.

.. 13 Mulberry trees growing wild on a summit.

.. 15 A rivulet.

.. 10 The rivulet of Sidero Kastro, along which the

·· 10   road runs through a narrow pass, almost choaked with shrubs, till it is recrossed at When ascend the steep hill of Sidero Kastro.

·· 15   Village of Sidero Kastro,—32 houses. The castle of St. Isidoro. The ruined fortress is 855 paces from the village; to this the ascent is rugged, and there is no prospect from the summit. Cape Katacolo bears NW. by N. The city of Arcadia SW. by W. ¼ S. Mt. Vourkano, or Ithome, SSE. The inhabitants of Sidero Kastro are barbarous, and not accustomed to the sight of strangers. A single kettle is the only utensil in the cottages. The winter is cold, from the vicinity of the mountains. Somewhere in the neighbourhood of Sidero Kastro must have been the cities of Dorion and Aulon, and, not far distant, Ira. The last was built of small stones, and hastily, like Sidero Kastro. There are two other ancient ruins between Sidero Kastro and Paulitza, on the mountains.

3 40

SIDERO KASTRO TO PAULIZZA.

H. M.

- ·· 25   From the village of Sidero Kastro to the further extremity of the castle hill.
- ·· 12   Cross a brook. Gennedi.
- ·· 21   Ascend in a valley. Village Ripesi r. A cave and fount l. Mt. Kurto N.W. Cross a rivulet.
- ·· 24   See Aito, a large village on the mountain above the city of Arcadia, bearing S. by W. Cross a stream.
- ·· 11   Village Kara Mustapha half a mile distant r.
- ·· 2   A summit. A beautiful and picturesque country covered with woods. The road is very bad after rain. See, l. village of Platania.
- ·· 15   After a dangerous descent among distorted oaks, are cultivated fields.
- ·· 7   In a valley pass the foundations of a tower, and vestiges of habitations. A road l. to Platania. L. see Cape Katacolo and Zante N.W. At Platania are the ruins of a fortress.
- ·· 11   A ruined chapel. Waterfall, Drymæ, l. The source of the stream is near.
- ·· 17   An eminence, ascended by a miserable path. A ruined fountain on the descent. Open groves, under which corn is produced.
- ·· 4   Foundations of a circular tower r.

H. M.

.. 4 On the banks of a beautiful stream running into the Neda. Enter a narrow glen, only admitting the path and stream. Dark groves of ilex platanus and laurel. Cross the brook.

.. 11 The dell unites with another; before which, cross the ruins of an ancient wall.

.. 11 Recross the main stream, and ascend by a very winding path.

.. 8 Glen again contracted. Pass a beautiful cataract shaded with laurel.

.. 5 Masses of fallen rock make the path very dangerous. Beautiful dell.

.. 30 After a very perilous zig-zag descent, recross the stream near a lime-kiln, and pass the Neda, now called Bousi, by a bridge with one lofty arch: nothing can exceed the grandeur of the banks of this river. The magnificent white precipices of the Neda are mentioned by Pausanias as one of the characteristics of IRA, in this vicinity.

.. 2 A rivulet and waterfall seen falling into the Neda r.

.. 15 After a steep and rugged ascent, pass the wall of an ancient city.

.. 5 Village of Paulizza.

4 0

LEONTARI (BY MACRYPLAI) TO KHAN OF SAKONA.

H. M.

·· 15 Having descended, with the castle r. on a peaked rock, and passed r. a ruined chapel, and l. the village of Kallidea, or Kallithea, cross the wide bed of the Xerillo Potamo, which rises out of the branches of Taÿgetus at Akoba and Kamāra, up the valley l. and joining the Alpheus in the plain r.

·· 5 Village Psamari, with its palaio kastro r. The valley of the Xerillo Potamo l. is beautifully wooded. On the right it is bounded by the lofty mountain Ellenitza.

·· 7 Fine oak woods.

· 3 Cross a mæandering rivulet.

·· 5 Forest at the base of Mt. Ellenitza.

·· 9 Ascend in the forest. The glen l. is called Pornarou Rema, or " of the prickly oaks."

·· 12 A top. The hill slopes to r. On Mt. Tetrage, or Tetrazi, see r. the village of Isari, or Isa-rāge.

·· 3 Heaps of large stones cross the road, as if there had been anciently a wall of defence.

·· 13 The road from Tripolitza to Arcadia, Andrut-zena, &c. falls in from r. Ascend in it through a narrow and picturesque glen.

·· 9 R. observe a tumulus or cairn of stones, called

H. M.

Της Γραιας ορος, which may mean the limit of the Arcadians and Messenians, or have been constructed in memory of the recovery of Orestes. It is 46 feet in diameter.

·· 30 R. near the road, a rock in the forest, supposed by the peasants inscribed, but in reality only covered, with lichen, in forms in which a fanciful resemblance to Turkish characters has been imagined.

·· 9 A patch of cultivation. Woody hills. A stream runs hence to the Alpheus.

·· 1 Descend in a beautiful and winding glen shaded with trees. Mount Vourkano, or Ithome, seen. A stream runs southward on l. having received a brook from r. L. of this descent is a palaio kastro, called Cochla, where are many ancient and modern ruins. Mr. Linck found a grotto with a curious basso rilievo, and heard here a tradition corresponding with the story of Amphœa. In this district is said to be a palaio kastro, called Suli.

·· 25 A derveni, to guard the pass. See the sea near Coron. Beautiful woods.

·· 5 Derveni of Macryplai. The plants are, sage, squills, coronilla, wild olives, almond, and filarea.

·· 25 Quick descent. Here the trees begin to be green on the first of March.

·· 33 After a very long descent, cross the brook

H. M.

from l. and arrive in the plain of Messenia,
or the Stenyclerian plain, and khan of Sakona, surrounded by a hedge of prickly
figs.

3 29

ARCADIA.

	H.	M.	Computed Miles.
38. PAULITZA. Phigalia.			
39. Paulitza (by Graditza) to Bassæ	2	22	. . . 4
40. Bassæ.			
41. Tragoge to Androutzena . . .	3	10	. . . 6
42. Androutzena to Karitena . . .	5	43	. . . 10
43. Karitena, &c.			
44. Karitena to Ampeliona . . .	5	13	. . . 10
45. Ampeliona to the Top of Mount Tetrasi and Isari	3	50	. . . 7
46. Isari to Lontari	3	38	. . . 10
47. Sinano to Leondari	1	28	. . . 7
48. Megalopolis to the Fount of Alpheius	1	28	. . .
49. Krano to Sinano	2	47	. . . 8
50. Sinano to Karitena	4	2	. . . 8
51. Karitena to Tripolitza . . .	8	43	. . . 18
52. Karitena to Gortys, or Atchicolo	2	13	. . . 4
53. Ampeliona to the Top of Mount Diophorte	1	0	. . .
54. Diophorte to Karitena . . .	2	50	. . .

	H.	M.	Computed Miles.
55. Kariteno to Saracinico . . .	3	55	. . .
56. Saracinico to Anazyri	4	26	. . .
57. Anazyri to Agiani	0	44	. . .
58. Agiani to Tsuka	2	5	. . .
59. Tsuka to Katzioula	6	2	. . .
60. Katzioula to Vanina	2	43	. . .
61. Vanina to Tripotamia	5	46	. . . 12
62. Tripotamia to Stretzoba . . .	3	18	. . . 9
63. Stretzoba to Kirpini	3	58	. . . 9
64. Kirpini to Betena	4	33	. . . 15
65. Betena to Khan of Dara, or Tarah	3	5	. . . 10
66. Dara to Lykourio	2	45	. . . 5
67. Lykourio to Katzanes . . .	3	43	. . . 10
68. Katzanes to Kalabrita	4	20	. . . 10
69. Kalabrita to Megaspelia . . .	2	30	. . . 5
70. Megaspelia to Patrass	12	55	. . .
71. Tripolitza to Lontari, or Leondari	6	23	. . . 18
72. Tripolitza, Tegea, &c.	1	17	. . .
73. Tripolitza to Mantinea . . .	2	3	. . . 7
74. Tripolitza to Kapsa	2	25	. . . 8
75. Kapsa to Kalpaki	2	59	. . . 8
76. Kalpaki to Zaracca	7	41	. . . 12
77. Zarracca to Phonia	4	17	. . .
78. Kalpaki to Phonia	5	38	. . . 15
79. Phonia to Lycouria	2	29	. . .
80. Phonia to Zaracca Lake . . .	3	30	. . . 10

PAULIZZA. PHIGALIA.

AT Paulizza, which seems to have been the ancient Phigaleia, may be observed the entire and extensive circuit of the walls of that city, defended by numerous towers, some of which are circular, situated on rocky hills and tremendous precipices. One of the gates on the east is yet perfect, and is covered with stones approaching each other till they meet. The country is so rugged, that provisions must have been scarce when the city was populous. The village of Paulizza consists of a few mean cottages. In a church are the fragments of a small Doric temple, of fine white stone. In the church of the Panagia are columns not 2 feet in diameter, and in the walls are two opposite ranges, 16 inches in diameter, with an intercolumniation of 2 feet 2 inches. The two ranges are 3 yards distant. Before the church several blocks seem like the foundation of a temple. West of the village, on the heights, are terraces, from which the course of the Neda is seen, but the meanders of Pausanias are not very conspicuous; the ruins of Lepreum at Strovizzi are also visible. The height of the situation renders Paulizza very cold during the winter. The glen of the Neda, below the village, is not to be equalled in picturesque beauty; the stream, clear and rapid, after passing the bridge and a mill, enters a chasm, where it is difficult to trace, between terrible precipices, beautifully fringed with wood.　On the right bank were the towers of Phigalia, and on the still more lofty rocks on the left was an ancient castle.

PAULIZZA TO BASSÆ.

н. м.

·· 30 After descending from the Acropolis of Phigalia at Paulizza, reach Gradizza, a village with 20 houses and a pretty fountain, in a little cultivated valley.

·· 7 Having ascended a stony glen toward the east, find on a brow the ruins of an ancient edifice, which the peasants call a reservoir; it was anciently a bath. This is in the direct road from Paulizza to the columns.

·· 15 Descending cross 2 brooks.

·· 5 Village of Kato Tragoge, or Tragode, 6 houses, with a brook.

·· 7 Many platani, and the road almost impassable from the number of streams.

·· 13 Cross a furious stream (perhaps the Limax). A chapel under some platani in the water.

·· 5 Reach Upper Tragoge, where there is a tower prettily situated. The people seem rather barbarous, but a lodging may be had for those who wish to visit the columns or temple of Apollo Epicurius. The village of Sklirou, on the other side of the temple, is a few minutes nearer, but is not always inhabited.

·· 60 Temple of Apollo Epicurius at Bassæ, passing in the way a little triangular hollow, with a fountain mentioned by Pausanias not far

G

from the ruins. The whole ascent is beautifully shaded with oaks, but very steep.

As Gradizza lies far out of the direct road, and
the path is in a most neglected state, the distance of 40 stadia, given by Pausanias, may
possibly be correct in a right line, though so
much more time was occupied in the ascent
than is usually employed on a distance of 4
miles.

2 22

BASSÆ.

THIS is the ancient name of a spot celebrated for the temple of Apollo Epicourios. It is now only known by the name of " The Columns." This magnificent ruin is now known in England as that whence the beautiful Phigaleian frieze was carried. The situation is a ridge, between two higher summits, covered with ancient oaks, on one of which, but as yet undiscovered, was a temple. Pausanias mentions one of Eurynome not far distant, at the junction of the rivers Limax and Neda, which has in vain been sought for. The temple at Bassæ is about 125 feet in length, and nearly 48 in front, and has 15 columns in the flanks, with 6 in the fronts. In the interior, which was hypœthral, or an open court, Ionic semi-columns have been applied as facings to several projections from the wall of the cell, forming a range of recesses on each side; these columns supported the frieze, which is now in the British Museum, representing the Battles of the Centaurs and Lapithæ, and of the Greeks and Amazons. The side opposite the great entry had a single column in the centre, with a curious species of Corinthian capital. This temple stands only 13 degrees removed from north and south, instead of in the generally adopted direction of east and west. There is a magnificent view from the temple to Ithome and the Gulf of

Coron on the l. while to the r. is seen the Gulf of Arcadia and the Strophades. On the foot of the hill toward the east is the little village of Sklirou, about half way to Ampeliona, which is distant 1 hour 50 minutes. The mountain called Diaforti, or Lycæus, and that called Tetrazi, or Cerausios, are toward the east. Across the Neda, and south of the temple, is a village called Kacoletri, near which are ruins, which some think those of Ira, the capital of Messenia in the time of Aristomenes. This temple is one of the objects of the greatest curiosity now existing in Greece; it is constructed in a beautifully smooth and durable stone. The cave of Ceres has not yet been found.

TRAGOGE TO ANDRUZZENA.

H. M.

·· 25 Cross a stream from MT. COTYLION r. Steep ascent.

·· 5 Another stream, also shaded with platani.

·· 4 R. observe fig-trees and gardens of a more ancient Tragoge.

·· 6 R. the dip in Mt. Cotylion toward the temple of Apollo.

·· 7 Descend among forests.

·· 8 A stream.

·· 1 Another rivulet, and a fount, called Tou Kahlili Idris, near which is a church.

·· 8 Upon an eminence; whence descend, under beautiful oaks, with a stream.

·· 8 On another eminence see Vervizza l. in a valley toward the sea.

·· 6 Descend from another height.

·· 4 A pretty brook.

·· 8 See the castle of Phanāri over the nearer hills.

·· 5 A tumulus, or heap of stones.

·· 5 An eminence like the rest formed by a projection of Mt. Cotylion.

·· 10 Fount called Panoūra r.

·· 20 A brook. Green jasper with red stripes found in the banks.

·· 2 A rivulet.

·· 5 A rivulet.

·· 18 Another brook.

·· 5 Stream and fountain.

·· 5 On the summit of a dip in the range of hills bounding at a distance the vale of the Alpheus. A most extensive view. See l. the villages Sanalia and Upper Andruzzena. Another on a summit, Kouphopolo, from which is a view of Fanari and the Hellenic fortress of Nerrovitza.

·· 25 Enter the scattered village of Andruzzena. The houses, which are wretched, are prettily intermixed with trees. There are 300 dwellings.

———

3 10

ANDRUZZENA TO KARITENA.

H. M.

·· 16 Cross a brook from r.

·· 60 A brook shaded with platani.

·· 4 Robea, a ruined village r. with a stream. Foundations of a wall.

·· 10 Vestiges of an ancient wall. Road runs E.S.E.

·· 3 Brook and walnut tree.

·· 27 After a very rough descent, shaded by evergreen oaks, see fields of Indian corn, and reach the banks of the river Surtenà. Ruins of modern habitations r. See the ruin called Labda.

·· 10 Cross the Surtenà by a bridge of one arch.

·· 12 The river receives another stream from the mountains in a little triangular plain. R. on the hill, is a village, Beleta. In this plain are the vestiges of a town connected with the ancient ruin called Labda on the summit of the hill l.

·· 1 Under a small rocky hill is the fountain of Labda. Above the source is a chapel and platanus. Surtena Panagia.

·· 22 See Karitena from a summit, with a church l. The road is bad. See the river Alpheus below. A beautifully wooded valley.

·· 73 Reach the Alpheus, after a dangerous and rocky descent. A stream falls in on l. Pass a mill. The road here turns r. ascending a most romantic glen, with a branch of the river, which suddenly ends by the mountains closing.

·· 12 The road turns l. across the head of the glen above a rock, at the foot of which the whole river gushes at once from the mountain. The spot is most beautifully shaded with platani. Above, r. is Tragomano. Some ancient vestiges on the spot.

·· 22 After a long ascent, the church of St. Athanasios.

·· 15 Ruined mosque, fountain, and modern remains.

·· 15 Chapel on a hill l.

·· 18 A garden r. The road turns l. to the bridge of the Alpheus.

·· 23 Bazar of Karitena, after a steep ascent from the river.

―――

5 43

KARITENA.

From Karitena the distances to the places
in the vicinity are thus estimated by the inhabitants :

3 30 To Steminizza.

4   0 To Dimizzana, a large town, with the most
flourishing school in the Morea, with a
library containing some old editions of
the classics. At Dimitzana is a palaio
kastro.

4   0 To Derstĕnà.

10   0 To Kirpini, or Girpini.

7   0 To Betena, or Vitina, a large village near the
ruins of METHYDRIUM.

8   0 To Tripolizza.

There are few, if any, vestiges of remote antiquity at Karitena. The ruined Venetian
castle is situated on a lofty rock, with magnificent precipices overhanging the r. bank
of the Alpheus. The name is probably derived from the vicinity of Gortyna; but if
any ancient town existed there, it was probably BRENTHEA, which must have been
very near the spot. It is scarcely possible
so fine a situation should not have been
selected for a city in ancient times. The

bridge over the Alpheus, with its chapel, is very picturesque. Lower down are caves in the rock near the river.

KARITENA TO AMPELIONA.

H. M.

• 15   Bridge of Karitena over the Alpheus. Road to Andruzzena r.

•• 40   Tiles under the Peak of Maureas.

•• 13   In a hollow under the Peak, a church and fount.

•• 4   A top. Peak r. Korognia village l. Ascend.

•• 36   Tiles.

•• 75   Karies village. 20 Houses with stone roofs. Many walnuts. A kastro on a pointed summit half a mile distant.

•• 60   A church and summit. A tower and some blocks. R. is Dioforte, whence there is a magnificent view, and the site of the altar of Jupiter. The road runs in a hollow apparently cut in the rock.

•• 23   Descending among fine woods, under which shepherds.and flocks.

•• 32   At the foot a river running into the Neda, which cross. R. on an eminence, a ruined city, with a fount and Doric fragments of white marble.

•• 15   Ampeliona, a small village in fine woods of chesnut.

From Ampeliona to Sklirou 55 minutes, thence to the temple of Apollo at Bassæ 55.

─────

5   13

AMPELIONA TO SUMMIT OF MOUNT TETRAZI.

H. M.

Quitting Ampeliona, descend, crossing a river; after which, a narrow, cultivated, winding valley runs into the range of Tetrage.

·· 52 A stream gushes out of the rock l. and soon after uniting with another rapid stream shaded with fine platani, runs toward the river Neda below. Ascend among bushes. This must be the real source of the Neda, called Hagno and Tetrazi. Mt. Cerausius. The source on the way to Tragomano must be that of the river Plataniston, which joins the Neda near Ampeliona.

·· 14 Scattered tiles and vestiges. See l. a ruined village, Rassōna. Forest of oak and platanus.

·· 94 Quit the direct road to Issari, turning r. toward the top of Tetrage.

·· 50 The road or path so bad that it becomes necessary to climb on foot.

·· 20 Top of Tetrage. Issara, or Issarage, is 2 hours distant from the summit. Magnificent view. Two churches, built of small ancient blocks of a stone not found on the spot.

———

3   50

ISARI TO LEONDARI (BY STALLA).

Descending from Isari, or Isarage, on Mt.
Tetrazi, or Tetrage, a pretty village. Pro-
ceed, without any road, in the direction of
Sinano, among woody valleys.

.. 56 Scattered tiles.

.. 6 A quadrangular plain. Stalla l.

.. 15 More tiles and vestiges.

.. 5 A citadel, now called Agios Giorgios, with a
church. This fortress has a precipice on the
side next Mt. Tetrazi. Karitena is called 4
hours distant. Here are ruins of small temples and fortifications of very ancient and
rude workmanship. Acacesium was in this
vicinity.

.. 2 Cross a stream running toward Sinano. Delli
Hassans Pyrgo, a large white tower, a quarter of a mile l. The building of this tower
has occasioned the destruction of many of
the marbles of Agios Giorgios.

.. 28 Tiles. The whole country exhibits traces of
an ancient population.

.. 16 Cross a stream. Sinano, across the Alpheus, l.

.. 8 Village of Dedir Bey.

.. 23 Cross a river from r.

H. M.

·· 29 A fountain.   A village r. and another l.

·· 25 A fountain.

·· 5 Lontari, or Leondari.   This Route is by Mr. Dodwell.

———

3 38

SINANO TO LEONDARI.

·· 3 Cross the ditch which surrounded the walls of Megalopolis, near which is a fountain and brick-kiln.

·· 20 L. is Mouzouza one mile, and Risvan Aga, whence comes a brook.

·· 11 Chioze l. across a vale. Cross a brook from it. The plain is in part woody, partly pasture and tillage.

·· 9 Cross the Megalo Potamo (Alpheus), and continue near its bank. Village Chamutze half a mile to l. on a hill.

·· 6 Ascend; Camara village, seen 2 miles distant.

·· 9 Woods. Chamutze near on l.

·· 5 A church l. Below, on the r. Kocheridi, east of which is Psamari, and its palaio kastro. Trees, tiles, and fragments. River Xerillo, a wide torrent, r.

  25 Town of Londari, or Leondari, after a steep ascent.

Leondari is a little town, governed by a Turkish waiwode. The mosque was once a Greek church. The situation is commanding, and terminates the chain of Mt. Taygetus on the north. In the area of a modern castle, in ruins, above the town, are the remains of several chapels; but no traces of antiquity are

visible on the spot, which has nevertheless
been taken for Belemina in Laconia, though
that place was 90 stadia from Megalopolis.
A Turk at Leondari is the owner of a pyrgo
at Sinano, where he will permit strangers to
lodge.

MEGALOPOLIS TO THE FOUNT OF THE ALPHEIUS.

II. M.

·· 20 From Sinano cross a brook. After it a church, with vestiges of a temple, 20 feet broad. The triglyphs are 11 inches wide, and 1 foot 8 inches high: metopes, 1 foot 7 inches broad: columns, 1 foot 9 inches in diameter at the base; at the top, 1 foot 6 4/10 inches. Here are also semicircular Doric columns.

·· 2 Cross a brook to Risvan Aga, a small village.

·· 24 Chapoga village, on a hill. Vestiges and tiles below it.

· 6 Cross a brook.

·· 4 A well.

·· 2 Kalybea.

·· 15 Vestiges on an eminence, and ruins of a little monastery, Palaio Rapsomata ; and a well. Hence a road runs l. 2 hours to Marmora, a village, 2 hours distant from the khan of Francobrysse, at Asea.

·· 15 Fount of Alpheius, in the plain of Megalopolis, mentioned by Pausanias, and seen from Palaio Rapsomati. This is in the western foot of a mountain now called Chimparou. The lake which produces it is in a plain on the north side of the hill, and is crossed by

H

H. M.

a bridge below the village of Anemoduri, in the road from Tripolitza to Lontari.

---

1 28

KRANO TO SINANO.

Krano seems to be Kromon, or Cromi, near which was the river and village of Gathea : west of it 200 stadia was a place called Nymphada, having many fountains; and in the same direction, 20 stadia more distant, was the Hermæum, on the confines of Messenia and Arcadia. This Hermæum was something more than 40 stadia from Megalopolis, or 15 from Phædria, which must have been in the pass below Isara, or Isarage, as through it went the road to Carnassia, of which place some ruins now existing near Constantino may mark the site. The position of the Hermæum would make it probable that Mount Tetraze, or Tetrage (CE-RAUSIUS) was not within the territory of Megalopolis.

·· 12   Top of the ridge between Arcadia and Messenia, with a forest of oaks. Mount Berbeni is seen above Leondari.

·· 15   Very ancient traces of foundations, with tiles ; from which descend, with oaks.

·· 35   A more steep descent conducts to the plain.

·· 40   The village Dedir Bey r.

·· 10   The Alpheus. Village Koremi a mile distant.

H. M.

·· 10 On the opposite bank of the shallow ford of
the Alpheus.

·· 23 Aias Bey, a village on a mount, and walls.

·· 22 Sinano.

——

2 47

SINANO TO KARITENA (BY DELLI HASSAN).

II. M.

·· 34	See l. the village of Aias Bey.
·· 12	Cross the river Alpheus. R. Rasseni, another village, between it and the river Helisson. A brook r.
·· 20	Cross a river from l. falling into the Alpheus.
·· 5	Delli Hassan, a new white pyrgo, built with marbles brought from an ancient city near Stalla. L. on an insulated hill, are probably the ruins of Acacesium. Pretty woods and hills under Mount Lycæus. Descend again toward the Alpheus. This is the road which Pausanias seems to have taken to Lycosoura, which must have been either on the remarkable peak called Sourias to Kastro, or almost on the summit of Diaphorte, near the Hippodrome, where are the ruins of a fortification, with towers and a fountain.
·· 15	Vestiges near the road on r. These may correspond with the site of Macareus.
·· 21	Cross a great stream. Vestiges near it, perhaps Dasea, on the smooth hill l. Bromosella, at the junction of the Alpheus with the Helisson and Aminius, r.
·· 16	Cross a brook in the plain
·· 12	Cross a brook.
·· 7	A great heap r. perhaps a tumulus.

H. M.

·· 9 Village of Cyparissia, where are the remains of an ancient city, with a fine fountain and walls. Probably Basilis

·· 16 On the opposite branch of the Alpheus observe vestiges, and 2 churches. Possibly Tocnia.

Between Cyparissia and the foot of the range of Mount Lycæus, or Diaphorti, is the village of Maurias, or Mabrias, near which is a valley now called Bathi Rema, or the Deep Glen, where the natives assert that fire often issues from the earth, near a fountain. The same story is told by Pausanias, who calls the place Bathos.

·· 40 The hill of Karitena begins across the Alpheus, and the stream Brentheates falls in from the north. L. a village called Florio, nearly corresponding with Melpea, an ancient village.

·· 13 Bridge of Karitena.

·· 22 After crossing the bridge, a steep ascent to the Bazar of Karitena.

———

4   2

KARITENA TO TRIPOLITZA.

H. M.

·· 10 On a plain.

·· 15 Churches r. and l. Cross a stream called Cha-
libachi.

·· 17 Delhi Hassan and Bromosella both seen to
the r.

·· 7 A high flat.

·· 21 A brook.

·· 4 Vestiges to r. and a tumulus.

·· 15 Mountains come close on r.

·· 5 Brahimi r.

·· 13 Palaio Suli.

·· 17 Palaio Paula, and a well.

·· 55 A hollow.

·· 17 Ascend the hills forming the boundary of the
plain.

·· 8 Palaio Paulo, or Palaiopoli.

·· 50 Ancient road.

·· 9 A glen, called Langadia.

·· 15 A tree, called Chrysokomereo.

·· 36 Derveni and khan.

·· 29 A plain to l.

·· 7 An old derveni.

·· 28 See Doulia.

·· 5 Gallipaki and Davia are seen.

·· 30 Leave plain of Davia.

H. M.

·· 30   A summit in a glen.

·· 15   An aqueduct.

·· 30   An uneven plain.

·· 35   Arrive at Tripolitza.

_____

8 43

KARITENA TO ATCHICOLO (GORTYS OR
GORTYNA).

H. M.

.. 40 Turn r. near RHŒTEA, which was at the junction of the Alpheus with the Gortyna.

.. 25 Ascend by a rugged and winding path, after
passing the bridge of the Gortyna.

.. 35 Monastery and caves' below the road r. in the
rock.

.. 13 Temple of Æsculapius and ruins called Marmara. Gortys.

The ruins of the temple of Æsculapius consist
chiefly in a platform about 90 feet long by
45. There is a second temple, once an oracle
of Apollo, among the ruins. The walls (of
polygonal masonry) and gate of the city remain; it was small, but strongly situated in
a wretched rocky mountain upon a tremendous precipice. Hence the summit of Dioforti bears S. 41 W. Peak of Maureas S.
22, 30 W. Village of Atchicolo N. 87 W.
Village of Marco N. 11 W. The river Gortyna, or Atchicolo, runs from a plain beyond Dimizzana, a town seen from Gortys.
The hill and town of Steminizza bears N. 66,
30 E.

1   53

AMPELIONA TO THE TOP OF MOUNT DIOFORTI, OR LYCÆUS.

II. M.

Proceed S. 78 E.

·· 15 Ascend from the ford of the NEDA, or one of its branches joined by the river of Agios Sosti. The sides of the mountain are covered with thick woods of chesnut, under which the shepherds of the country feed their flocks.

·· 35 Kastraki, or ruins, on the mountain. On an eminence is a single large tree, under which is a chapel. A fair is held here in May. Vestiges of a modern village. In a ruined chapel, near a source and an ancient wall, is the angular triglyph of a Doric temple, the frieze of which is 1 foot 2 inches in height. Here is also a fluted pedestal and a plain column 1 foot 9 inches in diameter. Large antique vases have been found here.

·· 10 Proceeding without a path, and passing a fountain among the bushes, by a very rugged ascent reach the summit of Mt. Dioforte, leaving in the way a valley on l. where there is a fountain said to be warm; this has been supposed that called Hagno, or the source of the Neda, in which the infant Jupiter was washed. The summit of Mt. Dioforte is a circular level, about 50 yards

H. M.

in diameter, evidently artificial; sacrifices
were here offered to Jupiter Lycæus: it
commands a most magnificent view over
the plain of Megalopolis, as well as that
of Messenia; while on the other side are
seen the hills of Elis. The modern city of
Arcadia, Cyparissia, bears S. 64, 30 W.
Mt. Tetrage S. 34, 30 W. Mt. Vourkano
(ITHOME) S. 25 W. Sinano (MEGALOPOLIS)
S. 55 E. Agios Elias (MT. TAYGETUS) S. 17,
30 E. Caritena N. 62, 30 W.

NOMIAN MOUNTAINS.—MOUNT DIOFORTI TO KARITENA.

H.   M.

Descending to the E. from the summit of Dioforti, observe at

·· 10   Several large and well cut blocks of stone, with the ruins of a Doric temple of white marble. The columns are singular in having 21 flutes, and are 3 feet in diameter.

·· 10   Below this, in a little plain near the summit of the mountain, are the ruins of a hippodrome; at one extremity of which is an edifice composed of two sorts of masonry, polygonal and horizontal. On the bank which forms the hippodrome are some stone columns. On the same plain, in the way from the hippodrome to Megalopolis, are the ruins of a fortification, near which is a fountain.

·· 30   From this valley, which appears like a crater, after ascending a little to N.W. a very rugged path and rapid descent runs near two sources to the village of Tragomano; the prospects are magnificent, extending beyond Elis to the north-west: but the account of time can of course give no precise idea of the direct distance over a precipitous country.

·· 50   From Tragomano to the source of a river

H. M.

rising at once from the rock and running into
the Alpheus.   A very steep descent through
a beautifully wooded country.

·· 20   Chapel of St. Anastasio on a hill; soon after
which, pass on l. the ruins of a mosque, and
see Caritena.

·· 35   Bridge of Alpheus near Karitena.

·· 15   Karitena.

2 50

KARITENA TO SARACINICO.

H.	M.	
1	5	Cross the bridge of the Atchicolo (GORTYNA).
··	17	Ruined village of Psoumourra.
··	18	Junction of the Gortyna and Alpheus at a place anciently called RHŒTEA, some vestiges of which are seen across the former upon an eminence between the two rivers. The road lies on the right bank of the Alpheus.
··	17	Opposite to the junction of the Tragomano river with the Alpheus l.
··	13	Cross a stream from Raphti, a village on a lofty mountain on r.
··	55	See across the Alpheus l. on a hill, the ruins called Labda. Turn r.
··	50	Small village of Saracinico, containing only ten houses, with a very pretty source; above are the ruins of another village, having also a fountain, and exactly opposite are the remains of Labda. Rafti is said to be 1 hour distant from Saracinico.

3 55

SARACINICO TO ANAZIRI.

.. 18   Cross a stream.

.. 60   On l. the ruins of an ancient city (Buphagus).
        On the right of the road, having passed the
        ruins, is a very fine source of the river Bu-
        phagus, with shady platanus, near which are
        vestiges of antiquity. Lower down upon the
        stream is a mill in a cavity which has been
        anciently made in the rock; this place is
        now called Trupe. The Alpheus here runs
        in a narrow, deep, and rocky bed.

.. 15   Remains of the modern village of Trupe.   A
        church r. under which is a fountain.

.. 12   Village of Matisi near the Alpheus l. Beyond
        is seen the high peak of Zakouka.

.. 18   Small village of Struzza r.   Quit the culti-
        vateable ground of Trupe, spotted with wild
        pear trees ; below, on l. are several trupœ, or
        caves, which gave name to the place.   De-
        scend to a plain.

.. 14   Cross a stream from Derstenà and Turco
        Raphti.

.. 26   Koccoura village r.

.. 30   A ruin and church dedicated to the Panagia.
        The ruin is that of a Roman bath, having
        a dome of brick, prettily covered with laurels
        and other foliage ; within it is a fine source,

H. M.

said to have been once warm, but now mixed. Melœnea.

·· 5 Vestiges of antiquity.

·· 10 Kakoreos, a chapel with stone columns of the Doric order with 16 flutes, diameter 15 inches.

·· 18 Cross a river from Ellenica. An ancient fortress on a hill r.

·· 20 A great source r. with beautiful platani and rocks.

·· 20 Village of Anaziri.

4 26

ANAZYRI TO AGIANI.

Anazyri, or Anaziri, is a small village, with a
pyrgo, where strangers may lodge; one hour
eastward, having crossed a ravine and two
brooks at their junction, an ancient ruin may
be found on the top of the steep hill, at the
foot of which the brooks unite; no columns
remain, but the foundations seem those of a
temple within a peribolus, whence the Doric
columns at Kakoreos in the plain below may
have been obtained; or here possibly might
have been a sort of citadel or castle dependent
upon Meloenea in the plain, where is a Roman dome of brick, noticed in the former
route to Anazyri. Near this Ellenic kastro,
as it is termed, is a little village, Papades.

·· 14   A river falls into the Alpheus.

·· 22   Ascend. In the way observe the circular
tower of an ancient city.

·· 8   The village of Agiani, or Hagios Iohannes,
consisting of a few huts. Agiani is situated
on the site of the ancient Heroœa of Arcadia.
The pretty eminence on which it stands pro-
jects from the hills which bound the vale of
the Alpheus on the north, and was protected
by a ravine on one side, with the river on the

other, near which are some baths. This city
seems to have been very respectable, though,
from the soil being cultivated, its remains are
few : buildings have here existed of the Doric order, but the columns now on the spot
do not exceed a diameter of 18 inches, and
are of a soft, porous stone : from the summit
a delightful view extends 20 miles over the
course of the river, across which, but toward
the west, is seen a hill called Palatia, from
ruins not Ellenic. A road went from Heræa
across the Alpheus to Alipheræ ; which fortress was perhaps that now called Nerrovitza,
nearly in the way to Phanari.

O 44

AGIANI TO TSUKA, OR TSOUKA.

Descend from Agiani to the Alpheus. See
the village of Pyri, or Peri, r. The banks of
the river are very beautiful, while the hills on
the north diminish to little eminences.

·· 28 The banks of the Ladon at its junction with
the Alpheus. The Isle of Crows mentioned
by Pausanias is seen at the mouth of the Ladon: it is a flat piece of ground, formed
by materials deposited by the river on the
spot where it separates into two channels
and unites with the Alpheus: it is often impassable. The hill of Palatia is near, and is
seen on the left bank of the Alpheus. The
Ladon was reckoned 15 stadia from Herœa,
and the Erymanthus 20 further. Across the
former, on the right, is a village on an insulated hill, called Belesh, or Belesi, somewhere
near which must have been the sepulchre of
Corœbus, the first Olympic victor. The distance between the two rivers occupies about
half an hour, and the road across both conducts to Palaio Phanaro, which seems the
ancient Phrysos, on a pointed hill.

·· 25 Having turned r. or north, proceed up the left
bank of the Ladon. Village of Memisi l.
Mirkinsi and Agiani r.

H   M.

·· 12 On a line with Belesh l.

·· 12 Ascend a bank.

·· 6 A fine view. Village of Scaniani seen.

·· 23 After passing a Turkish tomb l. find pretty woods.

·· 9 Cross a brook.

·· 10 Village of Tsouka, where there is a good house belonging to the secretary of a Turk, Arnaut Aga. The country is beautiful.

―――――

2   5

TSOUKA TO KATZIOULA.

H. M.

Quitting Tsouka, cross a stream.

·· 20 Cross a brook. Enter a green plain, between two streams. Se Renisi. This was particularly called "The Plain" by the Arcadians.

·· 6 A kalybea.

·· 29 Pyrgomachi, ruins of a town of undetermined date.

·· 10 Banks of the river of Langadia l. Enter a glen. Pretty fields.

·· 20 A river from r. joins the last. Tiles and vestiges.

·· 13 Huts l. below the road, and across the glen l. caves. R. the Langadia river.

·· 10 Mill below on l. and a road. A terrible and long ascent.

·· 35 Zulatica village, on a summit. Near it are fine rocks, with a beautiful and extensive prospect.

·· 19 Descending, pass a field, walled round, and apparently the remains of a very ancient fortress. Steep descent.

·· 13 A fountain of fine water, by a platanus. Some vestiges of buildings.

·· 22 Cross a brook from r. A river l. Fine scenery in a deep dell, with rocks and woods.

H. M.

·· 30   A mill and bridge. A river falls in from l.
A ruined village, Foscari, on a high rock l.

·· 4   Cross a mill-stream. A bridge and river. A
steep zig-zag road. Arachouni, or Rakouni,
on a height r.

·· 41   Cross a river from r. from Langadia, a town,
3 hours 30 minutes from Dimitzana, with 300
houses.

·· 15   Quit the river, which is probably the Teuthoa,
passing a wall of defence.

·· 35   Ruined village, Palaio Rachi, probably Teuthis. L. of this is a kastro, or fortification.
In a church a tablet of white marble, and a
column of 18 inches diameter.

·· 20   Descend and ascend to Galata.

·· 20   Village of Katzioula, a miserable place, in the
neighbourhood of a large ruined city.

6 2

KATZIOULA TO VANINA.

·· 14 Having passed a church surrounded with trees,
a fountain. Many tiles and ancient fragments.

·· 6 A church l. having passed another fine fount.
The church is called Agia Tryphona. Hence
a road runs l. to the kastro of Palaio Raki,
or Rachi, where is a Venetian tower : this is
presumed to have been the ancient Teuthis;
but a modern city has also existed on the
spot. The extent is considerable, and it was
entered by a sort of isthmus, by which it was
connected with the neighbouring hills. Here
are Doric columns of only 1 foot in diameter.

·· 10 Ascending, traces of ancient road.

·· 5 A summit ; whence descend.

·· 12 Village of Visitzi, a small place, but with
houses such as are seen in no other part of
the country, being larger and better built
than elsewhere.

·· 10 Having descended, a valley and vines.

·· 15 Descend in a glen, with a torrent l.

·· 7 A brook r. A fountain l. The road becomes
bad, and the descent steep.

·· 47 On the descent a fine prospect over the Ladon
and the Alpheus.

H. M.

·· 29   Cross a river, which runs from a perennial
kephalo brysso, or source.

·· 8   Banina, a kalybea of miserable huts, with a
palaio kastro, and very considerable ruins of
walls, colonnades, &c. Some of the edifices
seem quite unintelligible without excavation,
there being columns, fluted and plain, and
of several sizes and different intercolumnia-
tions, all placed near each other, but possibly
not in place. The view both up and down
the Ladon is beautiful, and that river merits
all that has been said in praise of its scenery.
Vanina is presumed to have been Thelphusa.

2 43

VANINA TO TRIPOTAMIA.

H. M.

Quitting the huts called Vanina, or Banina, in a beautiful situation, overlooking the river Ladon, on the left bank of which river the road lies, ascending in a valley, among delightful thickets and woods.

·· 18　Road to Spathari, the pyrgo or country-house of a very hospitable Turk, lying about half an hour up the hill r.

·· 36　After crossing a stream which falls from the right into the Ladon, where there are indications of antiquity which may possibly be the remains of the temple of Æsculapius, and the town HALUNS, pass the bridge of Spathari. This bridge crosses the river in a narrow pass between rocks : its high arch renders it dangerous but picturesque, and it has often suffered from the rapidity of this beautiful river.

·· 37　A station above a peaked summit overlooking the glen of the Ladon. This summit had a church called Agio Parasceve, with a castle. TROPHEI was a place somewhere in this vicinity. A steep ascent.

·· 24　Butzi on l. a wild but woody country. Some appearances of ancient habitation appear on the road.

H. M.

·· 18 Boccovina r.

1 21 Ascend to Velimaki, a large village, with a fortified house belonging to a Turkish aga. After the town is a very steep and zig-zag ascent, among firs.

·· 35 Top of mount; whence a steep descent to the valley of the Erimanthus. See Mostinizza, in a species of crater in a high mountain. In the village is the pyrgo of a good aga. The mountain is part of the chain of Olonos. Perhaps Pholoe, or Erymanthus.

1 10 A station, whence is a fine view of the vale, and the junction of the Erimanthus, Aroanius, and a third river, near the site of Psophis.

·· 25 Pass a bridge to the ruins of Psophis, with a khan built by a rich aga of Mostinitza, where travellers were once entertained gratis. The khan is between two rivers, one of which rises up the valley r. and the second, which is also crossed in entering Psophis, rises up another valley toward Sopoto. The description of Psophis by Polibius is very correct. This country is very cold in the winter. From the three rivers the place is called Tripotamia.

5 44

TRIPOTAMIA TO STREZOBA.

H. M.
·· 25 Alopcki, a village, on the hill l.
·· 15 Vestiges l. This road seems that of Pausanias through the Soronian wood, in his way to Psophis.
·· 10 Versiki l. 3 miles. Beautiful valley.
·· 10 Vestiges of antiquity. Fine scenery and woods.
·· 10 Village Dachouni r. and source of the river at the khan of Tripotamia: a source of error to geographers, who have made the river too long.
·· 13 L. vestiges, and great source r.
·· 9 Village Scupi l. on a rock.
·· 8 Church, and marbles. The valley opens on l.
·· 5 Cross a river joining the Ladon in another direction. Here is a mistake in D'Anville's maps, and all others. Palaio Kastro and great source l. This fortress has very curious remains of masonry, and it seems possible that it may be the PAOS of Pausanias. The source is very copious and beautiful.
·· 11 St. Anastasio village r. on a hill. There is a village called Nasos in this vicinity.
·· 22 Valley widens to a plain.

H.	M.	
..	48	Vestiges. Fine woods.
..	12	Strezzoba, a large village, beyond which a fine view toward the Ladon.
3	18	

STREZZOBA TO KIRPINI.

H. M.

·· 38   Vestiges.   After a descent, a beautiful valley.

·· 8   Podogora, a village of a Turkish aga; after which turn r. out of the vale of Stretzova.

·· 12   Wall, and Kastro on hill r.   An ascent.

·· 24   Top of the Kastro range.   Woods.

·· 26   Descend to Ladon river, and vestiges.

·· 20   Bridge of Kerasto, on the Ladon, r.   4 hours thence is the bridge of Spathari.

·· 19   A very steep climb to a station, whence there is a fine view of Stretzoba.

·· 7   Another steep ascent.

·· 12   Still ascend.   Fine woods.

·· 12   A very comprehensive view of the course of the Ladon.

·· 10   A top, and see Glanitza in a crater.   Turn l.

·· 50   Village of Kirpini, on a high cold top.

3   58

KIRPINI TO BETENA.

H. M.

[These routes were so covered with snow in the month of March, that the time is no measure of distance.]

·· 35   See Glaniza r. On the road a small palaio kastro l.

1 15   On a summit, Valtisinico, with a castle, or Battasinico, a large village, with trees. The situation is very lofty, and is seen from all parts of the country.

——

1 50

VALTISINICO TO MAGOULIANA.

1 30   Karphochilia, a village, among trees.

·· 20   Magouliana, after a descent. L. of the town, on a summit, is a castle called Argyro Kastro : it does not appear Ellenic.

——

1 50   at an extremely slow rate.

MAGOULIANA TO BETENA.

2 0   Descend to a temple r. Palatia : the foundations remain. Methydrium, ruins of, between 2 rivers.

·· 53   To Betena, or Vitina, a large village.

——

2 53

H.	M.	
1	17	Vitina to Palatia.
1	45	Vitina to Alonistena.
1	30	Alonistena to Kapsa.
4	0	Steminiza to Chrysovichi.
1	30	Chrysovichi to Piana.
2	38	Vitina to station in plain of Dimitzana.

BETENA TO KHAN OF TARA, OR DARAH.

H. M.

.. 18   A gap towards Lebidion, or Lebidi. Descend all the way.

.. 15   Granizza near, and Lasto.

.. 15   Plain of Vitina ends. Argyro Kastro l.

.. 52   Angelo Kastro r. Road to Tripolizza r.

.. 55   Khan tou Despotou. To Kalpaki 2 hours 30 minutes. Sopoto is computed to be 5 hours distant.

.. 30   Bridge and khan of Darah. Source Geoush three quarters of a mile r. from the khan tou Despotou.

———

3   5

DARAH TO LYCURIO.

·· 10 Ascend. Quit Kalavrita, road turning r.

·· 10 Plain of Tara ends. A steep hill.

·· 43 Village of Pancrate near. A good station for a view of the three valleys.

·· 10 Pancrate village on a height. Descend a steep hill.

·· 35 Fine source of Ladon, and vestiges. In this river are caught the fish epistrophes, a kind of trout. The water sinks from the Lake of Pheneos.

·· 57 Modern Lycouria, a straggling village. R. is the road to Phonia.

———

2 45

LYCOURIA TO KATZANES, OR KLITOR.

H. M.

.. 51 Great source of the Ladon.

.. 19 Chelona Spelia r. Turn r. up the valley of the Aroanius, a narrow glen.

.. 26 Ruins r. on a rock. Lusi may have been in this vicinity. The ruins may, however, have been the peribolus of a temple.

.. 25 Mill. The valley is very beautiful and well wooded.

., 13 A station whence a good view. On the mountain l. high up, is a cave and chapel. There is a story of the daughters of Prœtus, which may apply to this spot.

.. 13 Another mill.

.. 22 Traces of an ancient road.

.. 13 Katzanes kalybea and columns. Katzanes seems a name for many villages in this country. There is a place called Mazi, which has also many kalybeas.

.. 30 Klitor river and mills.

.. 10 City, temple, ruins, and tombs of Klitor. The temple was on a high peak. Sopoto is further up the valley. Karnesi is a village near Klitor. Near the kalybea is a fine source.

3 43

131

KATZANES, OR KLITOR, TO KALAVRITA.

H. M.

··	15	Gorge and ascent. Fine view of Mt. Chelmos.
··	24	Prosina l. A stream below on r.
··	16	After a very long ascent, the peak of Chalmo r.
··	7	Still ascending, a mill and bridge.
··	6	Kastræa l.
··	17	Village of Baloush and peak of Chelmo r.
··	10	Village Kamako.
··	10	A station whence there is a fine view. Pass over a high plain with a lake l. R. the magnificent Mt. Chalmos, or Chialmos.
··	40	Village of Suthena r. A cold country.
··	15	Sudena village. The bark of trees used for tiles.
··	10	Road to Klouchines. R. a steep ascent. Pines.
··	15	Top of a mount. A high pass.
··	60	Descend, with a kastro r. which may have been the ancient Cynethæ.
··	15	Kalavrita, a modern town in a deep valley, whence there is a way by Goumanitza to Patrass.

4 20

Kalavrita to Lalla 14 hours; to Psophis 7 hours.

Tara to Kalavrita direct 8 hours.

K 2

KALABRITA TO MEGASPELIA.

H. M.

.. 17 Having passed along the vale of Kalabrita, a bridge.

.. 43 A rock of singular appearance on l.

.. 10 See village of Suvargo on the mountain r. 2 miles distant. The vale winds to the left. Among the magnificent rocks l. a cave.

.. 20 Having turned to r. cross a bridge.

.. 15 Valley, now become a glen, turns l.

.. 12 Cross a bridge below the monastery of Megaspilia.

.. 33 After a terrible ascent, arrive at the monastery.

This monastery is a building of considerable size, perhaps the largest in the Morea. The precipice above it cannot be less than 400 feet in perpendicular height. The entire edifice is so completely within the arch of a great cavern, whence the name is taken, that the neglect of the roof is of little consequence, except in the winter, when large icicles fall from the rock. The Albanians, during an invasion of the Morea, not being able to take the place, endeavoured in vain to throw down a great fragment of rock apparently poised on the verge of the precipice; while the stones they were enabled to loosen all fell beyond the front of the edifice. They are said to possess a charter from one of the Constantines, and some books, but seem unwilling to show either. Above the entrance are some remains of building, contemporary with the Greek emperors. The monastery (the lower story of which consists entirely of a magnificent cellar, full of great casks,) contains 400 monks, who till the neighbouring country, and make good wine; but the vines, in so cold a situation, are cut down in the winter and covered with earth. From the entrance an inclined pavement extends to a sort of portico, between which and the church are two new and handsome brass doors. The church is covered with fine marbles, but is dark, from the immediate vicinity of the rock, though illuminated by silver lamps. The pavement is mosaic. The refectory is large, and its table clean. The Hegumenos sits on a great chair at one end, the rest on benches. The monks distribute an engraving of the place, surrounded with little pictures of the miracles wrought there. They are hospitable to strangers, and have a separate house for their Turkish visitors. The spot is exceedingly curious and picturesque.

MEGASPELIA (BY KALABRITA) TO PATRAS.

[FROM DODWELL'S MS.]

H. M.

.. 31 After a very steep descent, cross a bridge.

.. 23 Mill and fountain.

.. 2 Recross the river, over a bridge.

.. 30 See r. the village of Kerpini.

.. 25 Enter the plain of Kalabrita. The palaio kastro l. on a summit.

.. 18 Bridge of 6 arches. Kalabrita l.

.. 4 Doric column and capital. A cave in the hill r. the roof of which is cut into compartments. Near this a church, and another sepulchral cave.

.. 5 A source and marsh. The road to Tripotamia turns off l. R. a metochi of Megaspelia.

.. 29 The foundations of an ancient wall, near the end of the plain.

.. 30 Having ascended, descend among oaks.

.. 15 Cross a bridge, after which is a fountain in a plain. Olonos seen l.

Crossing the plain, ascend through woods of oak and platanus.

.. 68 A fountain. This spot was formerly notorious as the haunt of robbers. The road is often in the bed of the stream.

.. 24 Tiles. This place was once inhabited.

H. M.

·· 18   Cross a river, which falls into the sea near Vostitza.

·· 68   A khan l. and a palaio kastro r. on a hill. The khan is perhaps called Gouminitza. The ruins have been taken for those of Tritœa, and are very extensive.

Crossing a river, and ascending to the village of Gusumistri, occupies about 20 minutes. The ruins are sometimes called St. Andrea.

·· 23   Cross a stream.

·· 77   Cross a river.

·· 22   Cross a river. A village r.

·· 60   Woods and mountains.

·· 66   Tiles, and a few cottages. Mount Boidia (PANACHAICON) r.

·· 27   Having passed a little cultivated plain, a steep descent, called the Makellaria, or Butchery.

·· 41   Cross a stream in the plain of Patras.

·· 69   City of Patras.

---

12 55

TRIPOLITZA TO LONTARI, OR LEONDARI.

H. M

·· 13   Having passed a brook running from r. in a cultivated but bare plain, with some eminences, enter a rocky glen.

·· 10   Having ascended, quit the glen. Barren and rocky moor. Road runs W. S.W.

·· 2   Cross a road now ruined. See r. on the hill, the aqueduct of Tripolitza.

·· 15   Cross a brook from r. inundating an ugly plain, terminating left in a marshy sheet of water, one of the receptacles of the Alpheus. R. half a mile, a village on the foot of the hills. Thana, with vestiges of Pallantium.

·· 21   Leaving the plain, ascend in a glen.

·· 11   A top.

·· 5   A glen and brook cross the road. A fount l. Ascend a steep winding hill with three roads, of different ages.

·· 17   Top.

·· 23   Having descended by a rugged road, a derveni, at which pay 5 paras. A ruin r. on entering a little plain 1 mile and a half broad. Caloiero Bouni. A great tumulus r. with a tree and some vestiges of antiquity. L. on a hill, a ruined chapel. The streams run S.W.

·· 30   The mountains close in on l. leaving a narrow marshy plain. The khan of Francobryssi r.

H. M.

    Close to it is the Francobrissi, or fount of the Alpheus, with a few blocks of stone.

·· 10 A marshy valley falls in from r.

·· 10 Cross a bridge over the stream from r. R. on a peninsular rock with a cave, a ruined church and single tree. The walls and ruins of the ancient city of Asea are on the summit. L. in the marsh, are the foundations of a temple. The country becomes prettier, and has copses of brushwood.

·· 25 Cross a stream from r.

·· 3 Cross Francobrysse. A mill l. Recross the river. The hills on l. recede.

·· 24 A well, having crossed over a marshy lake covered with wild ducks, by a long, low bridge. The water sinks in a katabathron, or abyss, and rises again at a place called The Fountains, on the south side of the mountain.

·· 7 Ascend a steep mountain.

·· 6 Village of Anemodouri l. Asea bears N.E. by E.

·· 25 After a very steep ascent, on which robbers sometimes post themselves, a large church of the Panagia. A fine view over the plain of Megalopolis.

·· 20 Descending by a zig-zag road, see l. a village, beyond which is a hill, seemingly the site of an ancient fort.

·· 5 Vestiges of modern gardens and habitations.

н. м.

··	25	Still descending, among oaks.
··	15	On a woody knoll. R. Rhapsomata.
··	20	Pass through the site of a small ancient city. L. a beautiful vale, with inclosures and a garden.
··	15	Cross a river from the vale l. R. a deep valley, with oaks.
··	4	On a ridge. Beautiful country.
··	3	Cross a pretty stream, and ascend toward Lontari, with a brook l.
··	19	After crossing a brook, Lontari.
6	23	

TRIPOLITZA TO TEGEA.

Tripolitza is the modern capital of the Morea,
and is the residence of the pacha, or viceroy.
The number of the inhabitants is supposed
to be about 20,000 ; but it is the coldest and
least agreeable situation in the whole country. It may be now considered the representative of the three cities, Tegea, Pallantium,
and Mantinea, which once stood in this
plain ; and from that circumstance its name
may have been derived. Pallantium, the
city of the least consequence till the Romans
adopted it as their mother country, is not far
distant, on the road to Leondari. Tegea was
at Peali, near the road to Argos.

Passing through an ugly but cultivated plain,
see r. the lake into which flow the waters of
the Alpheus, after sinking near Saranta Potami and re-appearing. There is in this lake
a katabathron for the discharge of its waters :
they rise again at Francobrysso, near which
was Asea, and fall again into a lake near the
village of Anemoduri, making their last appearance at a place anciently called The
Fountains, in the plain of Sinano, or Megalopolis.

H. M.

.. 45 A village l. and church upon an eminence.
Agios Sosti. R. 2 wells.

.. 15 R. of the road see Piali, or Pegale.

.. 1 Cross by a bridge a stream running to the l.
which loses itself on the road to Argos.

.. 10 An ancient church; at which place and Piali
the scattered fragments of the edifices of
Tegea are found. The fields are covered
with broken tiles and heaps of stone. In the
ruined church are inscriptions, broken sta-
tues, and ruins of the Doric, Ionic, and Corinthian orders. There are large marble columns in a field near the village, and a capital of the Doric order, of great size, at the
well.

——

1 11

TRIPOLITZA TO PALÆOPOLI (MANTINEA).

H. M.

The road lies along an ugly plain, without trees; the mountains on the l. being near: those on the r. toward Tegea and Mount Parthenius about 4 miles distant.

·· 8 Village Agio Gerti r.

·· 30 On the hills bounding the plain r. see the village of Mouchli, which some have mistaken for Amyclæ. Agios Demetri r.

·· 10 Arnaut Oglou village l.

·· 6 Vestiges of antiquity, and a hill projecting from l. into the plain, the natural boundary of the territories of Mantinea and Tegea. A wall ran across the valley.

·· 23 Wallachian village l.

·· 6 Cross a bridge.

·· 15 See r. the monastery of Tsipiana, on the mountain. In the way to it observe a branch of the plain anciently called Argos.

·· 25 Cross a bridge over the river Ophis, which surrounds the walls of Mantinea. The city was nearly circular, if not completely so. In the walls were 116 towers, with 7 gates and a postern, all of which remain to the height of from 5 to 10 feet. Near the centre was a theatre, 213 feet in diameter. The gates were approached by bridges; vestiges of three yet remain. Several foundations of small temples may be traced, of the Doric and Ionic orders. Heaps of rubbish, in lines, seem to mark the directions of the streets. At the point where the river Ophis, reuniting its two branches, leaves the walls, observe a mound, apparently that formed by Agesipolis king of Sparta to inundate the city. The river falls soon after into an abyss, or kata-bathron. N. of the city is a conical hill, with a monastery called Chrysouli. There is a solitary house in the ruins, by some said to be called Arne, which was the name of an ancient fountain now existing there. The ruins of Mantinea are very singular, and are of the age of Epaminondas. A line of little mountains separates this plain from that of Kalpaki, or Orchomenos.

2 3

TRIPOLITZA TO KAPSA.

[This road is the same at its commencement as that to Mantinea.]

·· 35 After a flat and ugly plain, the hills on the l. approach the road.

·· 15 Ruins on the foot of the hill, and the 2 walls which divided the plains of Mantinea and Tegea.

·· 10 Road to Mantinea or Palæopolis r.

·· 30 A bridge. The ruins of Mantinea r.

·· 30 A katabathron, where the streams of the plain fall into an abyss. The plain is remarkably level, and there is no gradation of uneven ground between the flattest part of it and the mountains, which rise from it at once to a great elevation.

·· 15 The plain ends, and the hills close in from r. and l. Ascend, in a valley.

·· 10 Village of Kapsa.

———
2 25

KAPSA TO KALPAKI.

·· 50   Having ascended between high mountains on the l. and a lower range of hills separating the plains of Mantinea and Orchomenos, see r. an opening, through which is the shortest road to the latter.

·· 5   A descent.

·· 35   Vestiges of antiquity. Quit the road to Kalabrita, and ascend.

·· 35   Lebadi, Lividi, or Lebidiou, a large village out of the direct road, overlooking the plain of Orchomenos. [From Lebidi, Davia is 5 hours, by Reuno, which is 3: to Betena, 4 hours: to Dimitzana, 10 hours: to Kotusa, 2 hours.]

·· 37   Having descended from Lebidi, and crossed the Kalabrita road, cross in the plain a long artificial canal, which has been cut to drain the ground running eastward. On a hill r. a tower. L. the village of Rousso. Some heaps, or tumuli, in the plain.

·· 17   The small village of Kalpaki, or Kallipachi. Below it is a fountain. A little above the village are the foundations and some of the capitals of a Doric temple of white marble. The summit of the hill on which are the

ruins of the citadel of Orchomenos is about
13 minutes distant. The city extended to
the plain on the side of Kalpachi, as the
walls prove. From the citadel is a fine view
of the two plains and the lake of Orchomenos, with some part of the plain of Tripolitza.
The mountains on all sides are magnificent.

2 59

KALPAKI TO ZARACCA.

[BY MR. DODWELL.]

H. M.

·· 15 Mill and stream r.

·· 5 Cross stream. Hills close on r. Village of Mures r. River called Sosteno, from a vill. Nudines 3 hours distant.

·· 18 Kephalo Brysse, at foot of Kochino Bouno r.

·· 15 Tumulus l.

·· 16 Church l. Cross a stream running to W.

·· 8 Kandyla monastery on rock r.

·· 12 Metoki of Kandyla.

·· 5 Kandili village, nearly deserted.

·· 14 Three water-mills.

·· 4 Cross stream, other mills. Plain of Kalpaki ends.

·· 69 Ascend. Top of mount covered with snow. No road. Descend.

·· 83 A plain. Village Skotini near, l.

·· 4 Two streams meet at a spot with Homeric vestiges.

·· 71 A well. A flat cultivated plain running N.E. and E. Traces of very ancient walls at foot of hill l.

·· 10 Quit plain and ascend to l.

·· 25 See Lake of Stymphalus, or Zaracca.

H. M.

·· 37 After a descent, ancient foss-way and blocks.
Cross a river.
·· 5 Cross other branch from Dugio.
·· 15 Arrive at Zaracca.
_____
7 11

ZARACCA TO PHONIA.

[FROM DODWELL'S MS.]

H. M.

·· 15 Having descended to the plain, the remains of a Doric temple and other vestiges present themselves.

·· 7 A great source, or kephalo brysso, with the remains of a paved road. The water of this source was probably conducted, under one of the Roman emperors, to Corinth.

·· 2 A cape l. runs into the lake.

·· 8 Ruins—fluted columns of white marble and stone. A modern tower, and the ruins of one of the largest churches in Greece. This place is called Kionia, or The Columns. Turn l. ascending. A fine wall; and, l. are the remains of a cell. Ruins of Stymphalus l. A precipice above the lake, with the ancient road and traces of wheels in the rock.

·· 18 End of the lake on l. A wall runs along the plain to the left. A katabathron l. R. is a circular hill.

·· 33 A river l.

·· 11 Cross the river.

·· 8 Three mills and a cottage at the end of the plain. Ascend.

·· 17 Village of Kastagna, or Kastanza, seen on r.

H. M.

·· 23   The top of the ridge.   Hence the sea may be
           seen toward the east, and the plain of Phe-
           neos west.

·· 32   After a long descent, a fountain.

·· 33   Village of Mossia, Moschea, or Sumusha.

·· 50   Having crossed the river in the plain, the vil-
           lage or town of Phonia.

----

4 17

KALPAKI TO PHONIA.

Quitting Kalpaki, turn into a ravine l. between the hill of Orchomenos and a very rugged mountain, following the bed of a torrent.

•• 8 Ruins of a wall across the pass.

•• 2 The vestiges of the ancient city end l.

•• 8 Village of Kallithea r. Below it, a tumulus of stones r. Enter a plain, with a lake, surrounded by mountains.

•• 15 A magnificent source, or kephalo brysse, upon the road, of which water issues from many apertures, and runs to the lake on the l. Turn l. across the plain.

•• 3 Tumulus l.

•• 26 The road to the lake of Stymphalus, Zaracca, and Kionia turns off r.

•• 8 Another beautiful fountain close to the road, from many apertures under the mountain bounding the plain on the north. Turn a little l.

•• 14 Ascend, turning r. Monastery of Agia Triada r. A most difficult and rugged ascent succeeds, conducted through a bushy glen shaded by rocks.

•• 40 On a summit quit the glen, and see a small lake l.

H. M.

·· 6   On another top.

·· 19   Descend in a very romantic and confined hollow, darkened by high precipices on each side. The road is overhung with trees, and the whole singularly gloomy and magnificent.

·· 46   Village called Geousa. Under the church is a beautiful source.

·· 25   A very even plain, after a long descent, with a tumulus.

·· 27   The mountain which had accompanied the road suddenly opens to l. and forms the boundary of the lake of Phonia.

·· 50   Having traversed a road conducted upon a magnificent mound, with the plain r. and the lake r. cross the river Olbius, or Aroanius. Mt. Zyria r.

·· 35   Quitting the mound, a monastery l. and road to Lycuria. On a rough hill r. the ruins of Pheneos ; after which, ascend to the town of Phonia.

_____

5 32

PHONIA TO LYKURIA.

Having descended into the plain from the town of Phonia toward the west, pass between the lake l. and a monastery on the foot of the mountain r. On the way observe r. a high peak covered with pines, on which are ruins.

·· 42 Blocks, seeming to indicate a fortification of the pass between the lake and the hill. Observe r. across the lake, the signs mentioned by Pausanias of the ancient height of the water, which are visible at the foot of the opposite mountains.

·· 34 Foundations of a wall of ancient blocks at the foot of the hill r. The road runs S. W. The katabathron, or abyss, by which the waters of the lake sink, l. Quit the lake.

·· 33 Having ascended by a steep path, among pines, reach the top of the pass. Here the modern jurisdictions of Corinth and Kalavrita divide. Descend by another steep road.

·· 40 Modern village of Lycouria in a valley, with some cultivation, enclosed by lofty hills.

The village is small and straggling. The time is here given from a memoir of Mr. Dodwell.

PHONIA TO LAKE OF ZARACCA.

H.	M.	
••	10	Descend to Old Pheneos l. The plain of Pheneos.
••	6	Cross the river Aroanius.
••	13	A Zeugalathio, or village, l.
••	9	Cross another branch of the river, or the Ol- bius.
••	5	Ascend the plain on r.
••	8	Village of Moshea.
••	11	On the top of the ridge; perhaps the Geron- tean summit.
••	31	Descend. Traces of a division wall.
••	5	Khan of Kastagni. Fine view.
••	34	Vestige of a temple l.
••	12	Ancient Herculean road, or fosse-way, across the plain of Stymphalus.
••	35	After ruins, the lake of Stymphalus, or Za- racca.
••	4	Katabathron l. where the lake sinks. It after- wards forms the fount of the Erasinus.
••	27	L. Kionia, near the ruins of Stymphalus. R. a fine mountain with pines. Several traces of walls on the road. An ascent from the lake leads to Agios Giorgios.

3 30

ARGOLIS.

		H.	M.	Computed Miles.
81.	CORINTH to Cleonæ	2	30	. . . 10
82.	Nemæa.			
83.	Nemæa to Krabata (Mycenæ) .	2	24	. . . 6
84.	Mycenæ.			
85.	Krabata to Argos	1	52	. . . 5
86.	Argos.			
87.	Lake of Stymphalus to Agios Giorgios	3	50	. . . 10
88.	Agios Giorgios to Argos . .	5	0	. . . 12
89.	Argos to Tripolitza	9	15	. . . 25
90.	Mantinea to Argos	7	20	. . . 20
91.	Tegea to Nauplia			. . . 25
92.	Mycenæ to Nauplia (by Barbitza)	3	20	. . . 10
93.	Krabata to Tirynthus . . .	2	30	. . .
94.	Nauplia to Tirynthus . . .	0	30	. . .
95.	Nauplia to Port Tolone . . .	1	0	. . .
96.	Nauplia to Lykourio	5	48	. . . 16
97.	Lykourio to Jero	0	46	. . . 2
98.	Jero to Epidauros	2	14	. . . 6

	H.	M.	Computed Miles.
99. Epidauros to Potamia . . .	6	10	. . . 16
100. Potamia to Damala (Trœzene)	2	30	. . . 7
101. Damala to Kastri (Hermione) .	4	30	. . . 9
102. Hermione, Didymo, &c.			
103. Methana.			
104. Methana to Epidauros . . .	7	24	. . . 16
105. Epidaurus to Corinth . . .	11	5	. . . 25
106. Sicyon to Corinth	3	0	. . . 9
107. Corinth to Cenchrea and Schænus,			
and back	5	34	. . . 15

CORINTH TO CLEONÆ.

H. M.

.. 10 Having proceeded west, cross a ravine and stream.

.. 10 Cross two streams.

.. 6 R. a great forest of olives in the plain.

.. 10 Quit the plain and gulph. Cross a deep ravine by a bridge. L. another bridge and house.

.. 4 Having ascended by a steep path, r. two tumuli, a stone quarry l.

.. 5 Having descended, cross a bridge and ravine.

.. 5 Rachani village r.

.. 10 Having ascended, descended, and crossed a river, recross it near a mill (Bujukli).

.. 25 Cross the same river. A mill l.

.. 30 Village of Omar Tschaousch. Cultivation and cypresses. The road lies sometimes in the bed of the torrent.

.. 5 Pass a mill. A plain, with several villages.

.. 25 Cross a torrent, after which the hill and ruins of Cleonæ. The Acro-Corinth bears from this spot N. 65 E. Near the ruins of Cleonæ the road turns r. to Argos, and l. to Nemæa.

.. 5 On the road to Argos a khan, behind which Mr. Cockerell found a ruined Doric temple,

H. M.

in Antis, with part of a statue, supposed of Hercules, to whom the temple was dedicated.

2 30

Nemæa, near the village of Kutchukmadi, is 1 hour 15 minutes distant from Cleonæ, or 3 hours 45 minutes from Corinth. On the road pass a fountain l. a metochi, a church l. and a tumulus; after which observe the caves which the Nemæan lion is supposed to have haunted.

NEMÆA.

At Nemæa are the ruins of the temple of Jupiter. Three Doric columns are yet standing. The breadth of the temple was about 65 feet, and the length more than double. It was hexastyle and peripteral. The walls of the Cella, Pronaos, and Posticus together 105 feet 2 inches in length : width 30 feet 7 inches. The columns of the peristyle, 5 feet 2½ inches in diameter: upper diameter 4 feet 3 inches. The Pronaos, 4 feet 6¼ inches in diameter. Height of the columns, 31 feet 10¾ inches : capitals, 2 feet ⅓ inch : entire entablature, 8 feet 1¾ inch. Height of the 3 steps, 3 feet 6¼ inches. General intercolumniation, 7 feet ⅓ inch : angular intercolumniation, 5 feet 10¾ inches.

On a tumulus, at a small distance south of the temple, are other remains of the Doric order, probably of the Propylæa of the temple. There are indications of the Nemean theatre at the foot of a hill not far distant, and probably vestiges of the Stadium or Hippodrome of the Nemæan Games might be discovered by an attentive search. The valley is surrounded by hills of inconsiderable height, and the waters collected in it run toward the Corinthian Gulf.

The large village of Agios Giorgios is not far distant, but Kutchùkmadi is the village nearest to the ruins.

NEMÆA TO KRABATA (MYCENÆ).

H. M.

.. 10 Turn l. quitting the little plain of Nemæa, and ascending in a gap between the hills by a very rugged path. L. many caves, supposed those of the Nemæan lion.

.. 10 See a mill and cottages l.

.. 25 Turn r. having fallen into the direct road from Corinth to Argos. A derveni, or guard-house, l. A very narrow glen or hollow, possibly the Tretum of the ancients.

.. 15 A fountain l. The glen opens, and on an elevation across the brook r. an ancient ruin, now called Ellenon Lithari. See r. the village Zacchari.

.. 8 A tumulus r. The glen opens still more.

.. 7 A derveni l. A torrent frequently crosses the road.

.. 7 Tracks of ancient wheels in the road.

.. 8 Cross the vestiges of a wall.

.. 8 Cross another wall. The rocks of this country frequently assume the appearance of rough masonry. See a tumulus l.

.. 11 A tumulus r. Beyond it a chapel, near the road from Agios Giorgios to Argos.

.. 5 Cross a rivulet. A tumulus l. Enter the plain of Argos, the castle of which is now seen.

H. M.

R. the village and ruins of Phiti, or Phytai, possibly the temple of Juno.

.. 30 Ascend l. to the village of Krebata, passing several tumuli near the ruins of Mycenæ. If the path is not easily found to the left, the Krabata may be discovered by proceeding along the plain to the khan, whence the road to the left is evident.

————
2 24

MYCENÆ.

NEAR the little village of Krabata are the ruins of Mycenæ, once the capital of Agamemnon, built by Perseus about 1300 years B. C. and ruined by the Argives after the Persian war, 466 years B. C.

Following the water-course of Krabata, one of the first objects worthy of notice is the Treasury of Atreus, a subterraneous dome, over which the modern aqueduct passes. Descending to the right, the door is found, and the enormous stone 27 feet by 16. The diameter of the dome is 47 feet 6 inches; the height about 50 feet. A door connects this with a smaller chamber. Observe the holes and brass nails all over the edifice.

Following the water-course, the citadel and gate of the Lions will be found. Observe on the way a tumulus r. probably another treasury; and l. below the aqueduct, is another edifice exactly similar to that of Atreus, the roof only having fallen in.

The gate of the Lions is the earliest authenticated specimen of sculpture in Europe. They are said to have been executed by the Cyclopes. The walls of the recess in front of the gate, though composed of hewn and squared blocks, have the defects in construction of the Cyclopian style, in which it was not thought necessary to place a stone of an upper course exactly above the junction of two others in an inferior range; consequently it frequently occurs that the vertical joint continues through two courses. The polygonal walls in the citadel of Mycenæ are such as have been repaired at a later period, and should not be confounded with the Cyclopian. There is a curious postern-gate to the citadel. Above is a fountain which supplied the city. The gate, and a variety of other objects, are well worth the trouble of excavating. Other gates, now almost buried, would probably afford curious information to an excavator.

KRABATA TO ARGOS.

.. 12 Descend to the khan in the plain. Near it some blocks.

.. 7 Vestiges of antiquity r.

.. 17 A church l.; and 150 yards l. a foundation of large stones, and fragments of columns, or of mill-stones. The Heræum was at about this distance from Mycenæ.

.. 24 A road runs l. toward a church. R. the village of Pesopode.

.. 15 Cross the bed of a torrent from Pesopode.

.. 2 A tumulus r. and a branch of the Inachus.

.. 13 The other branch of the Inachus, a very wide bed of a torrent, employing 3 minutes in the passage, near the ruins of a modern bridge, of which 3 arches remain.

.. 16 Foundations r. Farm-house and trees r.

.. 6 A little mount, or tumulus, with a chapel. Near this is a well. R. is a hill, anciently part of the city of Argos. The modern town is entered at this spot, of which the houses, or rather cottages, though straggling, are generally built in right lines. At the south end of the hill of the citadel is a theatre. The walls are visible on many parts of the hill, and are of very ancient construction. On the summit anciently called Larissa is a

H. M.

modern castle in ruins, upon ancient foundations. Under a circular tower is a very ancient inscription.

1 52

ARGOS.

THE modern Argos occupies the site, and retains the name, of the ancient city, but the citadel is deserted; as is the hill anciently called either by the name of Phoroneus or Aspis. At the southern extremity of the town is a large theatre, partly cut out of the rock by the Greeks, and partly restored in brick by the Romans. Above it is a chapel, where is an inscription showing it to have been the site of a temple of Venus. Below the theatre are some fragments of sculpture near a church; and at a mosque surrounded with cypresses are several marbles brought from the grove of Æsculapius at Iero. By a diligent search the walls of the citadel may be traced: they ran round the base of the hill, and up to the summit. On some of the stones of the most ancient part are inscriptions. Under a tower in the citadel is an inscription in very ancient characters, of which a copy is much desired. This citadel was anciently called Larissa. The present towers are modern, though often on old foundations. There is a very good specimen of ancient walling on the summit. It is not Cyclopian, though the Cyclopians are said to have assisted in fortifying the city. From the top is a fine view over the plain, reaching to Mycenæ, Tirynthus, Nauplia, and the Inachus, to the north and east; and to the south and east, the fount of Erasinus,

the marsh of Lerna, and the Alagonian lake. Half-
way up the rock of the citadel, on the east, is a monastery curiously perched on the rock. Near it is a
cave, probably that of Apollo, who gave oracles there.
The ancient city was very extensive. The modern
town, though generally consisting of cottages, is increasing, and contained nearly 4000 inhabitants in the
year 1809. The children at Argos are remarkably
troublesome and insolent to strangers. Nauplia, or
Napoli, is about 7 miles distant

LAKE OF STYMPHALUS TO AGIOS GIORGIOS.

H. M.

The ruins of Stymphalus, or Stymphelus, lie on the northern shore of the lake, near the village of Kionia, or The Columns. Kionia is on the foot of Mt. Zyria, or Cyllene. Near this village, on the east, is a fine source and still more east is the village of Zaracca, which now gives name to the lake. The waters run off by a katabathron, or subterraneous passage, and appear again near Argos, at the fount of the Erasinus, 200 stadia, or 20 miles, distant.

.. 20 Having ascended from the south side of the lake, descend into the valley of Skoteini, and find the walls of an ancient city, probably Alea.

.. 5 Cross a brook, the Xerro potamo running to r. toward Skoteini, a village of 100 houses.

.. 27 Ascending from the valley, in a hollow, a tumulus l.

.. 8 Descending, an anathema in the road.

.. 20 A large tumulus, surrounded and sustained by a circular wall of rough stones. This has been anciently cut through, from motives of curiosity, and may possibly be the tomb of Æpytus mentioned by Homer and Pausanias, agreeing exactly with the description

H. M.

of it by the latter. The mountain r. is called Platani.

·· 10 Having passed a well with traces of antiquity, and a rivulet, pass a tumulus l. with a chapel and a few old oaks. The country ugly and bushy.

·· 23 A dell, with a torrent running r. Koumariou Langadi.

·· 11 On a top, with a view over the plain of Agios Giorgios. Descend.

·· 36 After a very steep zig-zag descent, cross a brook, the banks of which are walled. Here are the walls and ruins of the city of Phlius. The cidadel was on the hill. R. two foundations of temples. A raised causey crosses the plain to Mount St. Basili r. Mount Gaurias, or Gabrias, r. with caverns near Abanitza. The city of Phlius extended half across the plain.

·· 12 Quit the walls of the city, turning r. across the plain.

·· 8 A wall. Mount St. Basili r. In the plain some cultivation. Cross a deep rivulet by a ruinous bridge.

·· 12 Several blocks on the point of Mt. Agios Basili r.

·· 8 Many more blocks of squared stone.

·· 10 Foundations of a wall.

·· 7 A wall from Mount St. Basili to the torrent. Here, in the chapel of St. Irene, are the fragments of a Doric temple.

H. M.

·· 3   Cross a brook running to l. on a bridge formed
by an ancient architrave.

·· 10   A church of St. Giorgio, with more Doric
fragments. Road to Argos turns off r.
Agios Giorgios, a large village, where excellent red wine is made.

___
3 50

AGIOS GIORGIOS TO ARGOS.

H. M.

Descend into the plain of Phlius.

·· 22 Cross a torrent running into the river of Orneœ and toward Sicyon.

·· 15 Having entered a defile, see r. a monastery of the Panagia, or Virgin, in a curious situation on a precipice.

·· 8 Heap, or tumulus.

·· 5 Cross a stream and traces of a wall.

·· 5 Cross another wall. Both these walls are found again in the route from Nemea to Mycenæ.

·· 5 R. a foundation seen across a brook.

·· 16 Tumulus l.

·· 2 Appearance of copper ore on the road.

·· 2 Several heaps of stone called anathemas, or curses, supposed to draw down upon some hated person as many misfortunes as there are stones in the heap. R. bushy mountains. L. a ruined chapel and torrent.

·· 15 Ascend. A conic hill l.

·· 5 A summit, with more anathemas. Very bad road, down a bushy glen.

·· 10 A stream and mill l. Road turns r.

·· 24 Cross a brook from r.

·· 6 Another road from Agios Giorgios falls in from l.

H. M.

··	5	Cross a valley and stream from r. Ascend.
··	15	On a summit, see Argos, Nauplia, and the sea. A road turns off l. to Phyti, where are ruins, probably of the temple of Juno, or the Heræum. Mycenæ is seen beyond Phyti.
··	13	Ancient walls l. near the road.
··	10	Ruins l. Plain of Argos.
··	42	Village of Pesopode.
··	27	Cross the river Inachus.
··	48	Having crossed the Charadrus, enter Argos.
5	0	

ARGOS TO TRIPOLITZA.

H. M.

1 0 Quitting Argos by the theatre, the road runs
in the plain, under the mountains anciently
called Lycone and Chaon, to the fount of
the Erasinus, or Kephalaria. Lerna l. Near
the fountain a deep cavern.

2 30 Ruin of a khan; near which is a broken column and some squared blocks. A fine view
back, over Lerna, Mount Pontinus, and Nauplia, with its gulph.

1 15 A khan. The road runs nearly W. Pass the
villages Agios Giorgios and Araithyrea (the
latter an Homeric name) r. near the khan.
The valley of Hysiæ.

4 30 Ascend by a very steep and zig-zag causey to
a summit; after which there is a descent
into the naked vale of Tripolitza, in which, l.
at Peali, are the remains of Tegea. Great
part of this route lying in the plains of Argos
and Tripolitza, the time employed may be
shortened without difficulty by those who
have no attendant on foot to 7 hours 45 minutes.

9 15

MANTINEA TO ARGOS.

H. M.

·· 45 From the ruins of Mantinea (Palaiopoli) to the plain of Chipiana.

·· 55 Monastery of Chipiana, on a mountain. It is 3 hours from Tripolitza. Steep ascent.

1 0 Summit of the ridge, on which gooseberry-bushes are found growing wild.

1 0 Village of Torniki.

1 5 After a very steep and zig-zag descent, the foot of the mountain.

2 0 Cross a large torrent.

·· 25 Across a plain.

·· 10 Argos.

This road from Tripolitza occupies the same time as the ordinary route, and the mountain road being both steep and bad, it is seldom used. It may, however, be eligible to such as wish to see Mantinea, on the way to Argos. The route is mentioned by Pausanias, who calls the mountain Artemisium.

———

7 20

TEGEA, (PEALI) TO NAUPLIA.

H. M.

1 30 Having crossed a part of the plain of Tripolitza, ascend to the village of Stenò, a place
visible from all parts of the plain, and so
called from its situation in a very narrow
pass.

Descend by the Scala Tou Bey, or the Bey's
Causey, from the Turk who made the road,
among fine mountains and bold scenery.

At the bottom of the descent is a torrent running to the Gulph of Nauplia.

Across the glen observe ruins like those of a
temple, and the spot is yet called Iero, or
Sacred, by the natives.

Cross the great road from Tripolitza to Argos,
at a khan in a valley.

Proceed down a long rocky slope, by the bed
of a torrent, to a cultivated plain on the
coast, south of the mills upon the Alcyonian
lake, near Lerna. After passing a point of
the mountain l. near a church and fount, find
the Alcyonian lake, still supposed unfathom-
able. It is now become a species of mill
dam, and turns certain mills, which give the
name of Mylæ to the spot. There are several houses here.

Proceed along the shore. L. is the Marsh of Lerna, formed by the rivers Phrixus and Erasinus.   In the sea are rocks, which being near the water's edge are dangerous.   They may have anciently formed the port of Temenium; the place is now called Scala, or the Landing-place. The road from Mylæ to Nauplia lies along the shore, and the distance in time is about 2 hours 30 minutes.

MYCENÆ TO NAUPLIA (BY BARBITZA AND THE
RUINS OF TYRINTHUS).

H. M.

      Quitting the citadel of Mycenæ, ascend be-
tween two mountains toward the west.

·· 5 A stone, under which rises the fount of Perseus.

·· 8 Vestiges of a wall and small ancient bridge.
Turn r.

·· 7 Top of the pass. A tumulus r. Descend to
south by a brook, having r. the peaked summit which is south of Mycenæ.

·· 20 L. a house. The valley opens. Mt. Arachne l.

·· 5 A church. Agios Demetrios.

·· 3 R. a large church of the Panagia, near which
rises a very fine roaring stream, which very
soon sinks into the ground. Four heaps r.
and one l.

·· 7 Cross the bed of a rivulet. L. a circular
mount.

·· 5 A small castle, on an insulated hill. A cave
near it.

·· 6 Chapel of St. George.

·· 4 A Roman octangular ruin of brick, probably
an edifice forming part of a bath, of which
there are other remains. Barbitza is seen on
a hill about one mile and a half distant l.
Above it is a cave.

H.	M.	
··	5	L. a heap of stones.
··	10	The road in the bed of the torrent. A narrow rocky glen. Kleisoura.
··	17	The glen opens into the plain of Argos. R. are ruins, on a projecting hill.
··	8	The plain, covered with stones, some of which have been collected into a large heap, 400 yards r.
··	20	A peribolia, or garden, r. L. on a hill, a pyrgo. Villages; churches; two wells, and the fragment of a column.
··	7	Two villages r.
··	8	Village r. L. a church. Ancient foundations r.
··	15	Three villages r. Pass through a village.
··	7	A church r. Cross a road from Argos to Epidaurus. On hill l. a church and tumulus. L. rocks. Enter a grove of olives.
··	3	Ruins of Tirynthus, and a well.
··	30	Enter Nauplia, having turned r. at an angle of the bay.

| 3 | 20 |

KRABATA (OR MYCENÆ) TO TIRYNTHUS.

[FROM DODWELL'S MS.]

п. м.

·· 8 A khan, with a fountain, at the foot of the hill of Mycenæ.

·· 13 Vestiges of antiquity on the road.

·· 26 Blocks of squared stone.

·· 3 More remains.

·· 2 A ruined church, in which are Doric columns, with their capitals and large painted tiles: the capitals are of a singular form, 2 feet square; the column has but 15 flutings; the upper diameter is 1 foot $6\frac{8}{10}$ inches, while another measured only 1 foot $5\frac{4}{10}$ inches.

·· 3 Another church, with many ancient blocks; a Doric column here has 16 flutings, and is 1 foot $6\frac{7}{10}$ inches in diameter at the top. Here is a well, and two oblong mounds of earth.

·· 7 Village of Phonika, where is a well, with fragments of the Doric order.

·· 18 Village of Aniphi, with a few olives; the plain is well cultivated.

·· 10 L. Platanista village: here is also a church, and Doric capital.

·· 15 L. vestiges. Village Mebacca l.

·· 5 Square foundations, with blocks of stone r. and part of a plain stone column.

H. M.

.. 9 More blocks of stone l.

.. 7 Village of Cushi, or Kutzi. Village of Ko-
phina l. at the foot of two hills, on each of
which stands a church. Olives to the l.

.. 24 The ruins of Tirynthus : their circuit occupies
about 7 minutes; their site is about 40 minutes from Nauplia.

———

2 30

NAUPLIA TO TIRYNTHUS.

H.   M.

Nauplia is the best built city of the Morea, and the nominal residence of the pacha. It is situated on a rocky point, on which are many remains of the ancient wall. The port is excellent, and very defensible; the fortifications, though neglected, are in better condition than is usual among the Turks. On an island off the point is also a small castle. Above the city, at the summit of a very lofty rock, is the fortress Palamedi, reputed impregnable, but it is not unassailable from the east. The Turks pronounce the name Napli, and Anapli: the Italians have given it the name of Napoli: the Greeks, pronouncing the *u* as a *v*, say Navplia.

Passing out of the gates of the city, with Palamedi r. under which observe a cavern, and several pretty kiosks and gardens, with the port l.

·· 15 Turn l. A pyrgo r. also a church and village, in a valley.

·· 7 A vale r. the sea l.

·· 8 The walls of Tirynthus, on a little rock, having passed a well in the plain.

Tirynthus was built for Prœtus by the Cyclopians, architects from Lycia, about the year

1379 B.C. The walls are nearly perfect, and the best specimen of the military architecture of the heroic ages, being generally 25 feet thick, and the construction, with their galleries, are well worth examining. The fortress is about 550 yards long, and about 80 broad. The general form is that of a ship, or boat, and had three entrances. A tower on the east side is 20 feet square and 43 feet high. The city was destroyed by the Argives about 466 years before Christ. It was frequently the residence of Hercules. There was a place called Sipeia near Tirynthus, and another named Mideia.

O 30

NAUPLIA TO PORT TOLONE.

H. M.

·· 6 The rock of the fortress of Palamedi being on
the r. the Bay of Nauplia ends, and the road
to Tiryns and Argos turns off l. Pursue the
road to Epidaurus, or Epidavro, turning off
r. toward the village of Giafferi.

·· 20 See a village, with a fountain and church l.
R. a large orange garden, or peribolia.

·· 9 Village r. on a hill. A chapel r.

·· 5 Farm-house and trees l.

·· 12 Church r.

·· 8 Village Giafferi, or Jafferi, with a pyrgo. A
village r. also a curious conical rock, under
which are two villages. A tower l. The
plain is 2 miles broad. Pass a village, and
ascend a steep hill by the sea. On this hill
are the foundations of an ancient town and
castle, of no great consequence, except on
account of the port of Tolone, which it over-
looks: perhaps Eione, or the Prosymna of
D'Anville. From the summit observe the
port of Vivares, supposed the ancient Asine,
and Drepano, a nearer port, perhaps the
Phlius of D'Anville. Near the coast is a fine
garden, with many trees, and a monastery is
seen on a rock projecting into the sea. Beyond Vivares, the capes of Krenidi and Ko-

rakia are seen. To the west lies the pretty
garden of Tolone, where the inhabitants of
Nauplia come to divert themselves on holi-
days. The islands Platia, Upsili, Specie,
and the rock of Haliusa, or Coronisi, are
seen. Port Tolone is formed by the rock
Macronesi, where is good water, and the
vestiges of a castle and monastery. There
is another dangerous and circuitous way of
returning to Nauplia, passing by the orange
garden, and climbing to a tower near a spot
called the Devil's Garden. The road is very
rugged. Pass the village of Karatone. In
1 hour 30 minutes from Tolone reach Laliote,
a house, and trees. At 2 hours from Tolone
find a large house, with trees, 2 churches,
and an orange garden. At 2 hours 6 minutes
the village Naria; and Napoli at 2 hours 30
minutes.

1   0

NAUPLIA TO LYKOURIO.

·· 6 Quit the bay of Nauplia.

· 14 A chapel l. R. an orange garden. L. a chapel, on a hill.

·· 10 Garden, or peribolia, r.

·· 5 Nairea, or Naria, r. beyond it Mirza. L. houses and olives, and a curious rock like a castle.

·· 20 Ascend from the plain, seeing r. the conic rock of Giafferi.

·· 11 Quitting the olive grove, the village of Katchingri, with a pyrgo r. Cross the deep bed of a torrent. R. a mount. L. village of Chinoparti. R. village Barberi, and a palaio kastro is seen.

·· 24 The palaio kastro r. beyond a torrent, on a bold rock : the walls are of ancient masonry. Agios Adrianos: probably Midea. A monastery behind it.

·· 8 Tiles, stones, and vestiges of habitations.

·· 12 R. a fountain. Ascend. Near a chapel and fig-tree, vestiges. L. a torrent bed.

·· 10 A brook, running to l.

·· 24 Across a wooded dell, the monastery of Agios Demetrios l. From the monastery there is another road to Lykourio.

H. M.

·· 18   A summit. The country deserted and bushy; the road is strewed with tiles.

·· 18   A valley, with heaps of stones. A brook runs to r. A tower r. of ancient Greek masonry. R. about a mile see a ruined palaio kastro, commanding the mouth of a glen, through which the brook runs to the sea.

·· 40   A brook from l. Mount Arachne r.

·· 22   A pass between the mountain l. and a castro r. of good Hellenic masonry, with square and circular towers, in excellent preservation. Descend among olives. A cave l. Many ancient traces.

·· 23   Village l. Cross a glen and a brook from l. A chapel, or temple, r.

·· 20   See Lykourio.

·· 5   A tower l. ruined, on an eminence.

·· 10   Glen l. running to Vivares, 3 hours distant.

·· 15   Vale, 2 miles wide. Fields, covered with stones. R. a fount and church.

·· 10   Many heaps, probably only to clear the ground.

·· 5   Church r. and Agia Marina l. with houses and a well.

·· 4   A road l.

·· 6   Chapel, or temple, r. A bridge crosses a stream from Agia Marina.

·· 8   Ascend to Lykourio.

5 48

LYKOURIO TO IERO.

H. M.

Lykourio is a large village, upon a hill once occupied by the town of Lessa, the walls and other vestiges of which are visible in many places. The great gate seems to have been in a place near the well. At the church of Agia Marina are 2 Ionic columns, and the foundation of a pyramid, or a tower, with inclining walls.

·· 10 From Lykourio arrive at the village of Peri.

·· 6 Village Koroni, a singular name, because the nymph Coronis was the mother of Æsculapius, whose temple was near.

·· 10 Turning l. enter a pass, anciently guarded by 2 towers.

·· 5 Cross a wall.

·· 5 Enter a triangular plain. R. 2 heaps of ruins.

·· 5 Many vestiges and stone foundations. Cross a brook from l. running out of the valley through a glen south. A temple and portico.

·· 5 Enter the sacred enclosure, or Grove of Æsculapius, now called Iero, in which are many ruins. R. of the entrance of the peribolus is the stadium, with 15 rows of seats. Near the entrance is a Roman ruin, evidently a sudatorium, or bath. Near this is a magnificent cistern, about 40 feet broad and above 100 long. These buildings are l. of the road. There is a smaller cistern r. Both appear of Greek workmanship, with Roman repairs, and were probably reservoirs, as the cement still adheres to the walls. The waterducts remain. Near the road observe the vestiges of a great temple, probably that of Æsculapius. There is also a circular edifice, or tholos, near it, S.W. of the temple. On the blocks of it are inscriptions relating the cures performed by the god. Near this are some beautifully sculptured marbles, and ornaments in terra cotta. L. of the road is the platform of another temple shaded by a large tree. The remaining pavement is about 65 feet long by 30 feet, having 18 slabs in length, by 8 in breadth. On the hill east is the foundation of another building. The theatre is visible from all parts of the enclosure, and is approached by crossing a deep ravine and torrent bed. It is one of the most perfect in Greece, the proscenium only having disappeared. The orchestra is 89 feet in diameter. Fifty-five rows of seats remain disposed in about 20 cunei. There seems to have been a species of naumachium to the east of

H. M.

the enclosure. There is yet a fountain, the
waters of which are reputed medicinal.

IERO TO EPIDAURUS.

Quitting the sacred enclosure, observe r. under a tree, the healing fountain of Æsculapius.

·· 5 Cross a brook from r. and observe foundations on the nearest hill r. Two rivulets run hence to the Argolic Gulph.

·· 3 The vale becomes a glen. Pass a stone wall. Descend.

·· 3 Another wall. Mount Arachne l. Cross a brook from r. and descend in a picturesque glen, with rocks and pines.

·· 13 Road from Lykourio falls in from l. Fine trees, and woods of arbutus.

·· 3 Foundation of a tower. The pass seems to have been much fortified.

· 16 Cultivation, and olives. Thickets of the arbutus Andrachne.

·· 10 The glen opens.

·· 7 See Ægina and Methona.

·· 6 Cross a stream from l. Myrtles. Beautiful scenery.

·· 10 Valley opens again. R. cultivation.

·· 6 Pretty fields. Olives and village l. under Arachne. Cross a brook from l.

·· 22 See a tumulus l. perhaps that of Hyrnetho. Soon after cross a brook. Roman ruins l.

II.   M.

··   2   A stream.

··   5   Cross the main torrent twice.

·   9   A cave l.   Ascend an eminence about half a
              mile from the sea.

··   14   Village of Pidavro, or Epidauro, consisting of
              a few huts, with a good port, formed by a
              bold peninsula, on which stood the city.
              Some walls remain, and on the isthmus a
              statue.   The temple of Juno was probably
              on a promontory west of the city.   The spot
              abounds in vineyards, as in the time of
              Homer.

2   14

EPIDAURUS TO POTAMIA.

H. M.

.. 8 Cross the torrent from Iero in a plain by the shore.

.. 4 Ascend a steep hill. Myrtle, arbutus, and juniper abound.

.. 68 Reach the top of the pass, now called Trachea. A most rugged road.

.. 13 Village called Koliates, in a rough valley.

.. 17 A dreary valley. Hadgimeto, or Aginito, with a well across a torrent r.

.. 25 R. a road falls in from Lykourio, distant 3 hours.

.. 3 Village Trachea l. An architrave and other vestiges here.

.. 4 Foundations of a small temple. A well. Cross a brook. More walls.

.. 13 Having crossed another brook, and seen a tumulus l. in a green and bushy country, with a valley r. through which runs a road to Adami, a road branches off r. to Krenidi.

.. 14 Having passed a tumulus r. on an eminence, see vestiges.

.. 6 Foundations and large blocks l. Cross a brook from Bedegni, a village l. Pass two little eminences, cross a brook, and see a tumulus r. Crossing another brook, see r. the distant mountains of Zakonia.

193

H. M.

·· 20 Descend in the same irregular valley. R. a pretty pastoral scene.

·· 6 Ascend, after crossing a brook.

·· 12 Another brook.

·· 7 Traces of a building on the bank of a brook. Village of Karatcha. Turn l. A few huts on a rock almost deserted. A path up a mountain leads from Karatcha to the sea. The road toward Potamia becomes a mere sheep-track, and is very difficult to find.

·· 15 Ascending a steep mountain. See l. a curious mount and cistern, under which is an arched passage, with a stone table.

·· 7 Cross a pretty brook.

·· 10 A fountain.

·· 43 After a tedious ascent without a road, among thorns, a summit.

·· 10 Descending rapidly, find a stream running toward the Gulph of Athens.

·· 10 A second brook, at the base of the conic hill, and ruined castle of Korasa r. The ruins seem modern. Cross a brook. L. a fountain. Still descending, cross another brook.

· 10 See the village of Potamia, and l. the Gulph of Methana.

·· 20 Cross a stream from a fountain l. Beautiful shrubs and oleanders.

·· 10 Cross a clear and rapid river in a romantic glen, with a mill.

o

H. M.

•• 15 After a steep ascent, the village of Potamia,
so called from its lovely river.   Potamia is
a large and very pretty place.   Entering the
village, cross a brook.

---

6 10

POTAMIA TO DAMALA.

H. M.

After crossing a brook, ascend to a point of the mountain.

.. 25 The road turns r. See the Isles of Calauria, Poros, and St. Giorgio. Descend.

.. 15 Cross a brook.

.. 5 A tumulus r. Cross a brook from r. Methana l.

.. 11 Cross a brook.

.. 4 Three brooks.

.. 10 Descend among trees by a brook.

.. 15 After a rocky descent, cross a rapid river running to the port of Methana.

.. 25 Foundations and large blocks.

.. 2 Village upon the hill r. L. another village, called Palaiouria. Cross a brook.

.. 11 A well constructed road, raised upon the foundations of the wall of the city of Trœzene. Cross a brook.

.. 5 R. the church of the Panagia Episkopi.

.. 22 Arrive at the village of Damala, having first passed a brook, a river with two mills, an ancient tower, and a beautiful orange-garden. Damala consists of 45 houses, and is the see of a bishop. There are several inscriptions, and some very ancient octangular columns of black stone. On the supposed

o 2

H. M.

citadel there are no antiquities, but from it is a fine view. The air is reputed unhealthy in the autumn. The port, anciently called Pogon, is formed by the promontory Methana and the islands Calauria and Poros. The church of Panagia Episcopi must be the site of the temple of Venus Katascopia.

2 30

Poros is a large town on an island of the same name, the ancient Sphæria, and is remarkable for its rocks of granite. It is only separated from the Morea by a very narrow channel, with a ferry, which is 1 hour and 30 minutes from Damala. The road lies in a plain, with mountains l. and the port r. The church of Agios Epiphanios is 30 minutes distant from Damala, and under it rises a fine stream. Half-way between Damala and Poros is the village of Paphia. The country abounds in oranges. At Poros mules may be procured, on which it is easy to pass over a sand-bank into the isle of Calauria, where is a large monastery, and the ruin of the temple of Neptune, where Demosthenes expired.

DAMALA TO KASTRI.

H. M.

.. 35 Reach a summit, after a very steep and dangerous ascent, crossing a brook at Damala, and thence ascending by a monastery on a high rock, near which is a fountain.

.. 39 A still higher summit, whence Hydra and many other isles are seen.

.. 6 An anathema. A road l. to Thermisi. Descend.

.. 40 Port of Thermesi l. Near it, on a rock, a ruined castle. At Thermisi was the temple of Ceres Thermesia. See the mills of Kastri.

.. 20 A rivulet in a dell r.

.. 25 See r. the village of Soukala. R. pass a large detached stone, under which shepherds and sheep shelter themselves.

.. 10 A pretty brook, called Sororo Potamo. Very bad road, overgrown with thorns.

.. 10 A bushy plain. Ruined derveni l. A brook from r.

.. 6 A chapel r. with blocks. Cross a brook. A road l. to Thermesi. Several indications of an ancient town in this plain, which is about 2 miles broad.

.. 7 Village of Eilio about half a mile r. It retains its ancient name.

.. 10 Pass more vestiges. Another road l. to Ther-

H. M.

 mesi. R. a road toward Potamia up a valley.

·· 17 Descend. L. across a dell, a fine fountain.

·· 17 Forest of Junipers.

·· 13 An uneven vale.

·· 5 Cultivation and trees. L. lime-kilns and several wine-presses.

·· 10 Having crossed a little plain bounded on the l. by a port, reach Kastri, the modern representative of the village of Hermione.

———

4 30

KASTRI, OR HERMIONE, DIDYMO, &c.

THE ancient Hermione was on the promontory below Kastri. The walls remain and many foundations of the temples. Neptune, the Sun, Isis and Serapis, Venus, Ceres, Bacchus, Diana, Vesta, Minerva, and Apollo, had temples here. Kastri is a town recently inhabited. The people speak Albanian, as do the inhabitants of Specie, an island not far distant, the ancient Tiparenos. There are two excellent ports at Kastri. Opposite is the large trading city of Hydra, on a small barren island of that name. Krenidi is 1 hour 30 minutes distant from Kastri, and has 600 houses. Cheladia is a village on the coast, 1 hour from Krenidi. Five hours distant is a village of 10 houses—Candia. At a port called Bizati may have been the city of Mases. Mases, Asine, and Halice are not yet discovered. Didymi is now called Didymo, and is near a lofty mountain of the same name, three hours from Kastri, in a northern direction. Mr. Hawkins found at Didymo a curious natural cavity in the earth, so regular as to appear artificial, and an ancient well with a flight of steps down to the water.

METHANA.

Quitting Damala, and proceeding toward Methana,

.. 15 Cross the bed of a river from r. Traces of a wall run along the road. A church r.

.. 20 The port at a small distance r.

.. 15 Near the sea are the ruins of a chapel, with an upright Doric column. The place is called Limne, and was probably the site of the temple of Diana.

On the hill toward Methana is the village of Masomata. L. is another called Tou Pasias. Palaiourea is a village on a hill near the isthmus of Methana. There are several volcanic productions in the peninsula: its modern capital is Dara, near which, on the coast, are ruins of the ancient city of Methana. The mountains are lofty and peaked.

O 50

DARA, IN METHANA, TO EPIDAUROS.

H. M.

·· 20 A fountain, having followed a track by the western shore of the isthmus of Methana.

·· 11 Village called Phallerini, in a small circular plain.

·· 13 The road lies on a bank of sand only a few yards broad, which now choaks the entrance of the Limani, or western port of Trœzene. Turn r.

·· 25 Pass over a promontory.

·· 10 A second cape.

·· 5 Cultivated plain, and village of Lessa.

·· 20 Cross the beds of two torrents. Lessa l.

·· 10 Plain of Lessa terminates. L. a lofty mountain, called by the people Ortholithi. It seems called Ipla by others.

·· 6 Ascend. R. a modern tower.

2 4 Village Phanari.

·· 10 Vines. Bare hills round a circular plain.

·· 10 Ruins called Palaio Kastro r. Several blocks. of squared stone in the plain.

·· 50 Cultivation.

·· 50 Village of Kollaki, or Koliates, l. noticed in the route from Epidaurus to Potamia.

·· 2 See Epidauros, or Epidauro, from a top of Mount Trachis.

H. M.

·· 58 After a dangerous descent, the vineyards in
the plain.
·· 20 Village of Epidaurus. [This route is by Mr.
Dodwell.]

___

7 24

EPIDAUROS TO CORINTH.

H. M.

1 15 Having ascended among pretty bushes, with
the sea l. pass a church and fountain.

·· 15 Village of Piada, surrounded by a pretty plain.
On a high rock is a Venetian fortress, overlooked by Mount Arachne.

·· 2 Cross a stream, turning a mill, r.

·· 18 A church r. Cross two streams, with mills,
and enter a little cultivated plain.

2 10 Ascend among olives to a long narrow plain,
among low hills.

·· 42 Turn r. quitting the plain.

·· 18 Pass Angelo Kastro, a large village, with a
ruined castle on a hill. Descend.

·· 30 Pass a well in a long, narrow, cultivated plain.
Another well farther on.

·· 25 The plain ends.

1 0 Village of Agiani.

1 0 The road from Agiani remarkably rugged.

1 20 Cross a torrent bed between rocky hills. The
port of Cenchrea, and the village of Mertese,
where vases are found, lie r.

1 10 Not far from the foot of the Acrocorinthus,
some ancient blocks. Cross a stream, leaving
Cenchres far on the right.

H. M.

·· 40 Arrive at Corinth. [This route is by Mr. Dodwell.]

―――――

11 5

SICYON TO CORINTH.

From Sicyon to Corinth the distance may be about 9 miles. The time may not be correct.

·· 13 Cross a river, over which have been two bridges : one has a fine arch of ancient work and large blocks standing. This river comes from the valley of Agios Giorgios and the ruins of Phlius.

A brook and four rivers are passed in the plain, all of which issue from the hills on r. The grove of olives is of considerable extent.

2 11 Ravine, and bridge over a river.

·· 10 Quit the olive grove. The range of the Acrocorinthus is near, on r.   Cross a stream.

·· 6 Two streams. A fountain r.

·· 10 Ravine and stream. A metochi l.

·· 10 Corinth.

3 0

Lechæum is about 35 minutes distant, on the coast l. and consists of about 6 houses, magazines, and a custom-house. East of it the remains of the port are yet visible, at a place where the sea runs up a channel into the fields.   Near it are the remains of a modern Venetian fort.

CORINTH TO CENCHRÆ.

H. M.

·· 30 Having left the road to Megara l. and passed
a teke with cypresses l. near which is still
further l. across a ploughed field, the ruin of
a fine amphitheatre, cut out of the natural
rock, cross a river from r. On the descent
to the stream ancient foundations.

·· 5 A road turns off l. toward Schœnus.

·· 5 A ruin l.

·· 10 Cross a brook.

·· 8 A garden, with a large house, and the village
of Hexamillia. From Hexamillia a road
runs to Schœnus, along which there are many
very curious ancient quarries worth seeing.

·· 14 Village of Xylokephalo r. at the foot of the
hills.

·· 6 A circular stone, and other vestiges. R. on
an eminence are polygonal walls.

·· 13 Vestiges of a wall across the road. Descend
gently. A hill l.

·· 18 Steeper descent in a bushy glen. L. a church.
R. a brook.

·· 9 Walls l. On the hills observe walls r. probably modern.

·· 17 A wall, and the port of Cenchræ, now Ken-
chres. A well r. about 6½ miles from Co-

rinth. Here is a custom-house and a magazine, belonging to the Bey of Corinth. Several blocks of granite form the quay : there is also a tower formed of ancient blocks. South of Cenchræ is seen a tower upon a rock, near which are the hot baths of Venus. Beyond this is another bay, and still more southward is the village of Mertesi, where curious vases are found. At Cenchræ, near the sea, is a curious sepulchral cavern.

1 14 Passing over ugly eminences near the Saronic gulph, reach the walls of the isthmus. Here is a stadium; and, within a ruined peribolus, the ruins of a Doric and an Ionic temple. Some travellers say there is a theatre, but the remains of it must at least be doubtful. On the foot of the hills toward Kinetta is a tumulus, which may be that of Melicerta, in. whose honour the Isthmean games were instituted. There yet exist traces of a canal, or ditch, carried from the port, or bay, of Schœnus, along a natural hollow at the foot of a line of fortifications. There are also several pits, which have been sunk for the purpose of examining the rock previous to cutting through the isthmus, which has often been in contemplation. The ground, however, is so high, that the undertaking would be one of enormous expense. This place is

Π. Μ.

also ill chosen for defence, as it is overlooked by Mt. Geranion, on which the fortifications should be constructed. There is a road to Kinetta, passing the sites of Crommyon and Sidus in the way, along the coast toward Megara. Beyond Kinetta is the Kaki Scala, anciently the Scironian rocks, and Megara ; but the way is neglected, and travellers usually go over Geranion, by the derveni, to Megara.

2　5　Corinth, returning in the direct line by the quarries.

———

5　34

P

LACONIA.

<table>
<tr><td></td><td></td><td>H. M.</td><td>Computed Miles.</td></tr>
<tr><td>108.</td><td>LEONDARI to Peribolia . . . .</td><td>4 57</td><td>. . . 13</td></tr>
<tr><td>109.</td><td>Peribolia to Papiote . . . . .</td><td>2 37</td><td>. . . 7</td></tr>
<tr><td>110.</td><td>Papiote to Mistra . . . . .</td><td>1 14</td><td>. . . 5</td></tr>
<tr><td>111.</td><td>Mistra to Sparta . . . . . .</td><td>0 52</td><td>. . . 3</td></tr>
<tr><td>112.</td><td>Mistra to Sclavo Chorio . . .</td><td>1 45</td><td>. . . 7</td></tr>
<tr><td>113.</td><td>Mistra to Krabata . . . . .</td><td>3 48</td><td>. . . 12</td></tr>
<tr><td>114.</td><td>Krabata to Saranta Potami . .</td><td>3 59</td><td>. . . 12</td></tr>
<tr><td>115.</td><td>S. Potami to Peali . . . . .</td><td>2 29</td><td>. . . 6</td></tr>
<tr><td>116.</td><td>Mistra to the Mouth of the Eurotas.</td><td></td><td></td></tr>
</table>

Routes in Laconia.

Routes in Maina.

LONTARI TO PERIBOLIA.

H. M.

·· 15 A church r. on hill. A. Nicolo. Limatero village l.

·· 4 Woods and rough fields. Road runs S. 20 E.

·· 13 After a beautiful grove a well, with traces of antiquity. A church of Agios Giorgios. On a hill other indications of a town.

·· 23 A brook.

·· 3 Vestiges of a city, and tiles. A person of the country called the spot Bourainos.

·· 8 A church r.

·· 7 A river. Traces of ancient road.

·· 3 A river, joining the last.

·· 2 A large tumulus of stones l. surrounded with trees and other hillocks. A stream accompanies the road.

·· 3 Strong stream from r. Mt. Cherasia joins the Mt. of Lontari.

·· 3 Cross a brook.

·· 1 Cross another, and the foundations of a wall l.

·· 13 Vineyards and mulberries.

·· 1 Many streams, and a ruined hut l.

·· 4 Descend in a steep glen. A church l.

·· 6 L. Mt. Chimparou. On Mt. Cherasia pines. A brook.

·· 9 L. church and vestiges. A river from r. joins the last.

·· 4 Brook from r. Fields and trees. Cross a path.

·· 7 Brook from r. in a vale.

·· 4 Traces of antiquity near a fine tree.

·· 6 A brook.

·· 3 A hill, like a citadel, projecting from Mt. Cherasia.

·· 5 After a brook, more indications of a city. Foundations, like temples, r.

·· 6 A brook, and platani 7 feet in diameter. L. is a ruined church, and a most beautiful and copious fountain. L. across the stream, a church and house.

·· 4 Cross the city wall, after which a brook, and more vestiges. A triangular valley l.

·· 5 A brook. The conic hill called Chelmo, or Chelmina, seen both from Megalopolis and Sparta, begins on l. More blocks. The continuation of the range of Mt. Cherasia, called Xerro Bouni, r.

·· 5 More vestiges, like a water-conduit. Beautiful fields and vineyards.

·· 6 A brook. Poplars. Summit of Mt. Chelmo l. Glen narrow.

·· 6 Descend from an eminence.

·· 4 Tiles, and a stream from r. Beautiful valley.

·· 7 A church r.

II. M.

·· 2 A great tumulus, in the centre of a valley. L. a village.

·· 3 A road to Tripolitza l.

·· 4 Cross a stream from r. and immediately after the Longanico Potamo, from the village of that name seen on the hill r. Both flow into the Alpheus, having been joined below the tumulus by a stream which seems to be derived from the lake between Francobrysse and Anemodaure. At the junction of the two streams are the indications of a temple.

·· 9 A brook. Stones l.

·· 2 A Turkish tomb r.

·· 2 A derveni. Pyrgo l.

·· 3 Fount l. in a narrow glen.

·· 8 A brook.

·· 7 Agios Basili seen on a high part of Mt. Cherasia.

·· 5 A summit. L. on a high hill, a church and tree. Xerro Bouni r.

·· 5 A tomb, or circular foundation. The vestiges of a city on a high table land, now Agrapoulo Campo. On this flat many stones and heaps, like tumuli.

·· 25 A narrow valley, after a descent from this plain.

·· 2 R. of the road a beautiful source (Cephalobrysso), with the foundations of a temple, and fragments of white marble. The source of the Ere river, or Eurotas (Pellane?). Near the fount a ruined khan.

·· 7   After passing a church r. cross the river Platanata, which joining the stream Cephalobrisso, is called the Ere, or Eure.

·· 11   Ascending, vestiges.

·· 5   Having descended into a plain, see l. Partali, on a hill. Houses l. Trupes.

·· 5   Fount, and walls. Poplars. A gate in the walls, which run up to a citadel rising in terraces r.

·· 2   Cross the other wall of the same city. Cross also a brook, and find a ruinous khan. The village of Peribolia, or Perivolia, is about a mile distant on r. should the khan be without a khangi, or keeper.

———

4 57

KHAN OF PERIBOLIA TO PAPIOTI.

II. M.

·· 3 A river from r. and Xerro Bouno. Foundations of a temple r.

R. village Alevrou, and a pyrgo (Kalitèa).

·· 5 Broken pottery, ruins, and a stream from r.

·· 2 Stream, and vestiges.

·· 3 Farm-house (Demirgè, or Demire).

·· 4 Gegore l. Cross a stream. L. a tumulus.

·· 11 A stream. Pass among little hills in the centre of the plain.

·· 4 A river.

·· 2 Chorithitza village l. and a white house (Lai).

·· 5 Stream, and poplars.

·· 11 Cross a great river from r. which unites with the Platanata and Cephalobrisso stream, and assists in forming the river Ere.

·· 8 Having entered a glen, and passed a torrent, see r. across the Ere two churches, on two conical hills (Agios Giorgios and A. Nicolo).

·· 12 Narrow glen of the Eurotas. On the l. bank walls of defence down to the water.

· 16 Having passed several islands, and a mill, the glen opens into a valley, about a mile in breadth. Cross a stream and an ancient wall across the pass.

·· 2 A great wall, and other vestiges.

H. M.

·· 6 Enter a glen. See l. a white house. Ancient road, supported by a wall. Oleanders, or rododaphne, possibly the roses of Sparta and Pœstum, 20 feet high.

·· 10 A pass, fount, and church. Fields succeed.

·· 5 Foundations l.

·· 3 Ascend.

·· 3 Aqueduct, and a semicircular valley.

·· 6 River from r.

·· 5 A white house seen across the valley.

·· 5 Bridge over a river from r. A Turkish tomb, a glen, and r. a cave called Fourni, with steps cut in the rock.

·· 3 A modern ruined aqueduct, and an inscription with the word or title Spartiaticos. A church l. with vestiges, beyond the Eurotas, and a stream. After this place a little plain.

·· 3 See a cave l. in a mount from r. only leaving a pass for the Eurotas. A wall, and aqueduct.

·· 6 Quitting the river, ascend to a tumulus of stones l. After which another, which seems natural.

·· 4 Enter a plain. Papioti village seen r. Terraces.

·· 10 Papioti, having passed a little marsh on l. R. a stream, and tiles.

2 37

PAPIOTE TO MISITRA.

From Papiote a road turns off l. to Sparta,
and another r. to Mistra. See across the
Eurota, l. a house called Ploka. A tower
lower down.

·· 8 See r. a ruined aqueduct. A valley, with
bushes of Salvia. A church and aqueduct.
A stream runs to the Eurotas.

·· 8 Pass an aqueduct of the lower ages l. consisting of a lofty pier, and two smaller, with
an arch. Perhaps intended to convey water
to Sparta.

·· 3 Turn out of the valley by a ruined modern
channel for water, and many oleanders. Mt.
Taygetus is in view in front.

·· 15 Turning more to l. and ascending, see Mistra. R. about 3 miles, see Troupœ on the
the mountain, a village famous for an enormous cypress, and very picturesque. Nothing can exceed the magnificence of the
first sight of Mistra.

·· 11 A temple l. after a descent. Cross a large
river. Ascend. Mills r.

·· 23 A church l. Cross a river.

н.   м.

·· 6   The lower houses of Mistra, passing a square
       enclosure, in which a fair, or panagyri, is
       held.

1   14

MISTRA TO SPARTA.

H. M

Mistra is a large city on the foot of Mt. Taygetus, governed by two vaivodes. It has
five parts: the kastro, or citadel of a lofty
rock, Meso Chora, Kato Chora, Tritsella,
and Parorea; and has a bishop with the
title of Sparta and Amyclæ. It is pretended
that it had once 20,000 inhabitants; while
nothing can exceed the beauty of the situation, with the river Pantalimona running
through the city.

·· 22   Leaving Mistra, cross the river, and find a
ruined pyrgo l.

·· 6   Cross the river Maoulia over a bridge, near
which are some houses.

·· 17   An aqueduct and ruins.

·· 7   A Doric metope. Enter the city of Sparta
by an ascent. The walls are of the lower
ages, and made of fragments of columns
and the blocks of ancient edifices united by
mortar. Here is a magnificent theatre, 418
feet in its longest diameter. The orchestra
is 140 feet wide; but the scene seems to
have been only 28 feet deep. Adjoining
are two parallel walls, which are about the
length of a stadium.

Sparta was situated upon hills of small elevation; the east side next the Eurotas being
naturally defended by a wall or precipice of
rock about 50 feet high. Over the Eurotas
was a bridge, of which the vestiges remain,
but of uncertain date; between this and
the city was a small amphitheatre, but
of Roman times. Beyond the Eurotas was
Mount Menelaion, a range of hills of little
elevation. South of the city of Sparta is
a bridge of one arch, of large uncemented
blocks, over the Tiasus, a river coming from
a place called Trupia, where there is a fine
cypress worth seeing; this river falls into
the Eurotas near a village called Psisichi.
The bridge is one hour from Amyclæ. Between Sparta and Mistra there is a fine
Turkish villa surrounded with cypresses.
There are also ruins of a Roman bath; and
at a church of St. Irene were some marble
fragments. Between Sparta and the Eurotas is a hollow, which may have been the
stadium, or hippodrome. The whole city
appears to have been about a mile long,
in which were included 5 hills; on the
fourth of which from the north remain the
foundations of a temple. Upon the hill near
the theatre is a ruin, of which the two entrances, though nearly buried, seem perfect.
An excavation there would probably afford
something interesting. The ancient road

must have passed near the Eurotas toward Papiote. The country is not always safe, being so near to Maina and Bardunia. A large stream, now called Tchelesina, falls into the Eurotas a little north of Sparta.

MISTRA TO SCLAVO CHORIO, OR AMYCLÆ.

H. M.

·· 36 Cross a river from Parorea, a village probably reckoned part of Mistra, on the hill r. The foot of Taygetus r.

·· 14 Observe an altar among the bushes.

·· 15 Village of Agiani, with a beautiful mosque and groves of orange-trees. A copious stream, or kephalo brysso, runs through the village.

·· 10 Agiani Cheranio, a Greek village, and church.

·· 10 A river, Tsoka, from a village of the same name on Mt. Taygetus r.

·· 10 A river and mill kephalo brysso. Village Kodina seen l. At the kephalo brysso, or source, is a church on the site of a temple. An Ionic capital of white marble, a stag and hounds well sculptured, a statue, and some architectural fragments, mark the spot.

·· 10 Village of Sclavo Chorion. At the distance of 3 hours r. on the mountain, is the village of Agia Sotera.

1 45

At Sclavo Chorio are many churches, and a few inscriptions; on one of which is the name of Amyclæ. The village is very pretty, with open groves of olives. There

are some Doric capitals, and other fragments, but the inscriptions of the Abbè Four-
mont never existed at Amyclæ. Proceeding
from Amyclæ toward the Eurotas, at the
distance of about 2 miles is a church on
an eminence, called Agio Kyriaki; having
passed in the way a pyrgo of Mahomet Bey
r. and the village of Kodina, with a church
and fount. From Agio Kuriaki there is a
fine view of the course of the Eurotas, near
the banks of which Mr. Gropius found a curious circular edifice, like the Treasury at
Mycenæ. Potamia and Daphne are also
seen to the south. On the west, the whole
range of Taygetus, and toward the north,
the theatre of Sparta, is visible.

MISTRA TO THE KHAN OF KRABATA.

н. м.

.. 11 Quitting Mistra, pass over a brook called Pantalimona. Hills begin to approach from the foot of Taygetus. A road to Trupe, or Trypai, l.

.. 4 A church r.

.. 4 Cross a brook running into the Pantalimona.

.. 3 Road runs in a hollow among little hills.

.. 3 A top.

.. 5 Another top. A pyrgo near, r. Descend.

.. 3 A church l.

.. 2 A river from Trupe in two branches. The Tiasos?

.. 2 R. in a field, blocks like those of a temple. A church near it.

.. 11 The last sight of Mistra. This road is the same as that to Leondari.

.. 15 A ruined aqueduct, with two ranges of arches, with a stream under it.

.. 10 End of the hill of Papiote, and another piece of the aqueduct.

.. 20 Having passed the little plain of Papiote, quit the Leondari road, and turn r. into the glen of the Ires, Eres, or Eurotas; cross that river by a fine bridge in a romantic spot, having passed a more ancient ruined bridge before it.

227

H. M.

·· 3 The road turns back a little, and a river falls into the Eurotas.

·· 13 Following the glen of the last river, ascend. R. across the stream, a rock with the appearance of antique vestiges.

·· 29 Boutiana village seen across the valley.

·· 19 A church r. and a stream l. Ascend from the valley of Boutiana.

·· 12 A fountain r.

·· 5 A fine stream runs to the Eurotas.

·· 1 A khan called Bourlia.

·· 9 Very bad road, on a summit. Descend. A church r.

·· 5 Vestiges. A few trees. Bare hills. A stream from r.

·· 2 A fount r. in a field.

·· 5 Vestiges r.

·· 5 A red mountain, Krabata, l.

·· 15 Stream r. of the road. See the river Tchelephina.

·· 4 A tumulus of stones r. See r. a fine mountain with pines (Gamako).

·· 8 Khan of Krabata. A road runs off r.

3 48

KHAN OF KRABATA TO SARANDA POTAMI.

H.   M.

.. 8 Ascend among bushes. A great tumulus r.

.. 3 Huts like those of the Turcomans, made of horse-hair by the peasants, on a shelf of rocks l. Ascend in a bushy glen.

.. 20 On a summit. R. see a great snowy hill in Zakonia, called Chrysapha.

.. 10 In the road a vein of ore. The place seems to be called Mangeri. The ore is like that of lead in powder, or emery, and is worth examining.

.. 8 Derveni of Batachi near on r. Tiles.

.. 6 On a top many stones, the ruins of a wall.

.. 23 A torrent running through an opening in the hills l.

.. 6 A little cultivated plain.

.. 5 Ruined walls. A hollow, called Tou Demetrios Laches.

.. 3 Ascend. Ugly country.

.. 12 Descend into a small plain.

.. 10 Ascend from the plain.

.. 5 A very narrow plain. Shrubby hills.

.. 15 Descend into a plain, in which is a brook of red water running toward the Alpheus.

.. 5 Large oaks.

.. 5 A little plain surrounded by eminences.

.. 2 A ruined church l. A small lake.

H. M.

·· 9   Tumulus of stones r. Quit the plain, and descend into a glen called the Kleisoura of Arracoba.

·· 10 Traces of ancient chariot wheels.

·· 6   Quit a little plain, passing the foundations of a wall of defence. Descend all the way.

·· 7   Very small triangular plain. Traces of habitation l.

·· 4   Cross a thick wall.

·· 3   Derveni of Arracoba r. Road r. to Agio Petro, distant 3 hours. Beyond the derveni a vale. Approach Mt. Berbena.

·· 20 Several heaps of stones l. Descend.

·· 3   Grave of a Turk l. who was murdered here by thieves.

·· 10 Glen shuts in, and turns l. Bed of a torrent r.

·· 10 Turn r. again.

·· 7   A tomb l. Winding descent.

·· 4   Derveni r. Near it the beautiful source of the Alpheus (Saranda Potami). Symbola. A stream comes down also from Bourboura, a village, 2 hours distant, upon Mt. Berbena r. Still higher, is the village of Koutrapha. Copious stream. At the derveni a wretched lodging for travellers may be procured.

3 59

SARANDA POTAMI TO PIALI.

H. M.

.. 14 Having crossed the river several times in a deep glen, with a rapid descent, a river falls in from l.

.. 5 Traces of a wall across the glen.

.. 10 Crossing the stream again, find another great wall. These were probably walls of defence between the Lacedæmonians and Tegeates.

.. 10 A ruin l.

.. 40 The glen contracts, and the river sinks into the ground. The mountains become lower, and the road is in the bed of a torrent. A pass between rocks. A cave r. the resort of shepherds.

.. 30 Quit the glen, which winds much. Enter the plain of Tripolitza, or Tegea. A lake l. into which fall the waters from Saranda Potami, or Alpheus, according to Pausanias. From this lake a katabathron conveys the water to to Frankobryssi.

.. 40 Having passed l. an insulated hill, pass over a little eminence, and reach Piali, a village on the site of Tegea, in the plain of Tripolitza. Piali is 8 hours from Argos, thus: to Agiorgitico 2 hours, Aklado Kampo 2 hours, a khan 1 hour, Argos 3 hours.   At Peali, by a well, is a large broken Doric capital, more than 5 feet in diameter.   In the village, other fragments of large marble columns of the temple of Minerva Alea.   At the great church are other fragments of the temple, and part of a long inscription.

MISTRA TO THE MOUTH OF THE EUROTAS.

[FROM GROPIUS'S MSS.]

AMYCLÆ, or Sclavo Chorio, 1 hour from which, near
the Eurotas and village of Baphio, is a treasury
like that of Atreus at Mycenæ.
Leuka.
Cross a stream from Taygetus r. falling into the Euro-
tas on l.
A village r.   Another seen l.
Cross to the east bank of the Eurotas.
A hill approaches the river from the east.
Cross a stream from l.
Ascend a ridge of the mountain, with a derveni.
The Eurotas flows in a confined valley between the
hill of the derveni and Lycobouna, a mountain of
the district of Bardunia, projecting from Mt. Tay-
getus.   The village of Daphne is in that territory.
Having descended from the derveni, the ruins of an
ancient bridge over the Eurotas.   The road re-
crosses to the west bank of the Eurotas, where
there is a village, and then returns to another village, on the east side.
A village seen l.
After passing an eminence projecting from Lycobouna
r. reach the village of Arabades.
Near a village the road again crosses to the west of

Eurotas to Scala, 1 hour from the sea, where there
is a beautiful source, and below it a mill. The
stream from Scala falls into the sea at Zacchari
Calamo.

After a village on the west bank, cross the Eurotas
near its mouth to a village, beyond which, passing
through six villages in the plain, the road to
Geraki, or Jeraki (by some supposed Geronthræ),
enters the hills. Jeraki is about 4 hours distant
from the mouth of the Eurotas. The marsh of
Helos is to the east of the mouth of the river,
and has several villages near its banks.

ROUTES IN LACONIA (OR MAINA) AND ZAKONIA.

[ESTIMATED BY THE NATIVES.]

MISTRA to Daphne, a place situated on a projecting branch of Mt. Taygetus, intercepting the view of the sea from Mistra, 5 hours.

Potamia, the capital of Bardunia, a lawless district, in the way to the sea at Helos, or Marathonisi, 4 hours.

Helos seems to be distant from Mistra 14 hours.

From Mistra to Calamata, over Taygetus.—To Pischino Chorio 4 hours. Pischino Chorio to Kutchuk Maina 6 hours, whence to Calamata 3 hours, a most dangerous journey, not only from the state of the road, but the perfectly lawless state of the country.

Helos to Marathonisi 3 hours. Above the latter is Mauro bouno.

Mistra to Bambako 10 hours.

Bambakou to Zakounia 2 hours. Zakounia was mentioned in the country as a village, but it is the general name of the eastern part of Laconia. Zakounia is 12 hours from Tripolitza.

Zakonia to Argos 12 hours.

From Tripolitza to Douliana (or Talliana) 3 hours,

passing the villages of Zeugalathio, Magoula, and Rizes.

Agio Petro is 5 hours from Tripolitza : a large town, in the district of Zakonia.

From Agiani to Astro 4 hours. Astro to Tripolitza 12 hours.

Agiani to a dogana and khan on the coast 4 hours.

From Astro, on the road to Argos, Andrutza 5 hours; whence to a khan 1 hour; to Argos 4 hours.

Andrutza to Skafidaki, on the coast, 3 hours. Scafidaki (by Mylæ) to Argos 3 hours.

From Talliana (or Douliana) to Kastri 1 hour. Thence pass through Platano and Prasto, near the monastery of Psaroma. From Prasto 4 hours to a kalybea of Prasto on the coast, and another of Korakobouni. Thence to Korakobouni 4 hours. Thence to Port Lenidi 4 hours. From Korakobouni to Astro 6 hours.

Mistra to Monembasia 14 hours. N. of Monembasia is an ancient city in ruins, supposed Epidaurus.

From Mavrobouni, near Marathonisi, 3 hours to Scutari, passing the village of Captain Antoni. Scutari to Vatika 3 hours, passing Kastri. Vatica is 1 hour from Kolokythia, supposed Gythium, the port of the Lacedæmonians.

Vatica to Vathia (or Bathia) 2 hours. Thence to Kastagnia 6 hours. Thence to Porto Quaglio 6 hours, which is a village named from the port 2 hours below it.

Porto Quaglio to Jalli 4 hours; 1 hour from Capo Grosso.

Jalli to Pyrgi 2 hours. Pyrgi to Cape Matapan (or Tænarus) 2 hours.

ACCOUNT OF MAINA,

BY THE BEY.

The villages of Maina, from Elios (or Helos) and the
mouth of the Ere Potamo (or Eurotas):

Trinisi, where are three islands.

Marathona, with the island Marathonisi, supposed
Cranae.

Passebos.

Porto Bathi.

Geranos, near the sea.

Tes Askamares.

Bourlachias, with temples of Diana and Bacchus.

Colokythia.   In the sea are ruins and inscriptions.

Porto Pagano, and Isle Scopes.

Leucadia, a castle above Colokythia.

Ampelo.

Porto Kallio.—The port of Achilles.

Cape Matapan, above which Kisternes, a castle, with
many cisterns.

Capo Grosso, ill pronounced by some Drosso.

Messapo castle and port.

Gimoba (or Dgimova).

Vitylo—Betylos.

Kialepha, half an hour from Vitylo.

Karotto Kastro (or Charia), on a hill near the sea.

Krio Nerro, 1 hour from the sea.

Kallies, 1 hour and a half from the coast.

Baccho, 1 hour and a half from the coast.

The road from Scardamoula (Cardamyle) to Chytries is so bad, that only mules can go upon it.

Near Scardamoula, on Mt. Calathios, a fine cave, mentioned by Pausanias.

The island Pephnos has yet two tombs, called those of the Dioscuri.

Kalamo, the ancient Thalama.

The country near Cape Matapan is called Kakaboulia. The Bey of Maina says there are ruins of a temple in Kakaboulia.

The whole district of Maina, including Kakaboulia, is formed by the branches of Mt. Taygetus (or St. Elias). This country has never been thoroughly examined by any English traveller, except Colonel Leake.

ERRATA.

Page 5, line 19, *for* sourie *read* source.
27 -- 3, *for* 6 18 *read* 6 19
45 -- 7 from bottom, *for* 4 6 *read* 4 12
70 -- 3, *for* Ciparissia *read* Cyparissia.
77 -- 4 from bottom, *for* 2 13 *read* 1 53
78 -- 7, *for* 5 46 *read* 5 44
78 -- 18, *for* Tripolitza, Tegea, *read* Tripolitza to Tegea.
78 -- 5 from bottom, *for* 7 41 *read* 7 11
78 -- 3 from bottom, *for* 5 38 *read* 5 32
83 -- 13, *for* hypœthral *read* bypæthral.
112 -- 2, *for* Melœnea *read* Melænea.
113 -- 13, *for* Melœnea *read* Melænea.
113 -- 5 from bottom, *for* Herœa *read* Heræa.
114 -- 11, *for* Herœa *read* Heræa
115 -- 14, *for* Herœa *read* Heræa.
129 . 1, *for* Quit Kalavrita, road *read* Quit the Kalavrita road.
161 -- 5, " left, the," *dele* the.

INDEX.

R

248

THE END.

Printed by S. Hamilton, Weybridge, Surrey.

For EU product safety concerns, contact us at Calle de José Abascal, 56–1°, 28003 Madrid, Spain or eugpsr@cambridge.org.

www.ingramcontent.com/pod-product-compliance
Ingram Content Group UK Ltd.
Pitfield, Milton Keynes, MK11 3LW, UK
UKHW010343140625
459647UK00010B/782